CW00459423

Fawkes — The Quiet Guy

A musical

Kjartan Poskitt

Samuel French — London
New York - Toronto - Hollywood

ISBN 0 573 08107 7

CHARACTERS

Matthew, **Eunice** — two servants
Catherine Wheel, the Mistress of Ceremonies
"Baby" James
Oliver, a Puritan sergeant
Maggie, **Jenny**, **Beth**, **Moll** — Chorus girls
Sir Robert Catesby
Father Henry Garnet, a Jesuit priest
Mrs Fawkes, **Mrs Percy**, **Mrs Wright** — old women
Thomas Percy
John Wright
Denise, a waitress
Sir Walter Raleigh
The King's Groom
King James I of England and VI of Scotland
Sir Robert Cecil
Lord Mounteagle
Dorothy, a chorus girl
Thomas Wintour
Sir Everard Digby
John Grant
Ambrose Rookwood
Chris Wright
Robert Wintour
Robert Keyes
Thomas Bates
Francis Tresham
Lily Gage, a mysterious woman
Bagwich, a servant to Mounteagle

Mary
Jack — members of Dorothy's family
Jane
Alice
Queen Anne, Wife to King James
Sir William Waad, Lieutenant of the Tower
Sir Richard Walsh

The Catesby's Cabaret **Chorus** and of course….

The Quiet Guy

See p. vii for notes re: doubling

FAWKES — THE QUIET GUY

First performed in York on May 13th, 1998 by Acomb Youth Musical Theatre Group with the following cast:

Catherine Wheel	Andrew Welch
Maggie	Beth Cowan
Jenny	Jenna Bell
Sir Robert Catesby	Adam Fletcher
Father Henry Garnet	Owen Gurrey
Mrs Fawkes	Rose Stephenson
Mrs Percy	Josie Mills
Mrs Wright	Nicola Brown
Thomas Percy	Matthew Brent
John Wright	Joe Stephenson
Denise	Lucy Pope
Sir Walter Raleigh	Joe Tavener
The King's Groom	Ben Chamberlain
King James	Thomas Brown
Sir Robert Cecil	Jack Thompson
Lord Mounteagle	Arron Dennis
Dorothy	Kirsty Brent
Thomas Wintour	Peter Smith
Sir Everard Digby	Josie Mills
John Grant	Simon Pope
Ambrose Rookwood	Rose Stephenson
Chris Wright	Joe Tavener
Robert Wintour	Beth Cowan
Robert Keyes	Jane Tavener
Thomas Bates	Carolyn Geraghty
Francis Tresham	Arron Dennis
Queen Anne	Sarah Stevens

Other parts were played by members of the company which also included: Anecia Jagpal, Kelly Souter, Charlene Pavis, Lauren Mitchell

The Quiet Guy played himself

Musical Direction: Helen Leach
Director: Doreen Gurrey

SYNOPSIS OF SCENES

ACT I

Scene 1	"Catesby's" Cabaret Club, night
Scene 2	Mrs Fawkes' living-room
Scene 3	"Catesby's" Cabaret Club
Scene 4	King James's Bedroom, night
Scene 5	"Catesby's" Cabaret Club
Scene 6	The Parlour
Scene 7	"Catesby's" Cabaret Club
Scene 8	Lord Mounteagle's House, Hoxton
Scene 9	The Palace
Scene 10	The Cellars

ACT II

Scene 1	The Tower
Scene 2	"Catesby's" Cabaret Club
Scene 3	Ingham Mote
Scene 4	The King's Boudoir
Scene 5	"Catesby's" Cabaret Club
Scene 6	The Tower Cells
Scene 7	"Catesby's" Cabaret Club

Maybe "Catesby's" Cabaret Club never existed — but everything in it did actually happen

Time — Between AD 1603 and 1605

AUTHOR'S NOTES

Character Guide

Most of the parts are fairly self-explanatory as they appear in the script, but here are one or two extra details which might prove helpful:

Catherine Wheel — the Club MC is brassy and shrewd — this part is suitable either for an outrageous woman or a man in drag.

Sir Robert Cecil — history has him as sinister and cunning. Physically he was quite frail with a distinct limp.

The Wrights — mother and sons are all strong Yorkshire stock, the brothers were noted as champion swordsmen.

King James — "The wisest fool in Christendom" — his tragic upbringing caused him to be quite paranoid and repulsed by all women apart from his wife. He could be friendly and charming, and yet unbelievably uncouth and sadistic.

Casting Suggestions

All but the very largest companies will find they have to double up on some of the parts. Although there are about forty named speaking parts, a company of twenty-five could perform the show in full using the following doubles:

Garnet/Waad
Jenny/Mrs Percy/Jane
Raleigh/Chris Wright
Moll/Lily Gage
Matthew/Jack
Walsh/Groom
Maggie/Mrs Fawkes/Mary
Beth/Mrs Wright/Alice
Oliver/Tresham/Mounteagle
Baby James/Eunice
Bagwich/Queen Anne/Denise

(Whether you are doubling up or not, the Chorus singing can come from anyone who is available.)

There are many other ways of doubling up the parts, and adapting them to fit your company — particularly if you have women playing some of the male roles (or vice versa). For the scenes involving lots of people, it isn't always necessary to have everybody on all the time, e.g. by letting Thomas Bates arrive late in a couple of scenes, he could also double with King James. If it helps to cut or re-allocate the lines of the smaller parts to make casting easier, then by all means feel free to do so.

Scenery

Most of the scenes are set in "Catesby's" Cabaret Club. A large sign at the back of the stage saying "Catesby's" should light to indicate when we are in the club, and at other times it should be unlit or obscured to suggest we are elsewhere.

All scenery is very minimal. Apart from the sign, the only essential prop to the club is a table from under which a person can enter and exit. All other furniture and fittings are listed in the text.

Historical Accuracy

Most people are aware of the story about the gang who planted gunpowder under the Houses of Parliament.

Guy Fawkes was discovered waiting to light the fuse and following his ghastly interrogation, the conspirators were all caught and executed.

Actually the true story of the gunpowder plot is far more complicated ...

It directly involves over twenty leading characters along with hundreds of other people, and the issue is further confused by the fact that many of the relevant details were suppressed at the time and will probably never be uncovered. A typical example of this is the confession of Thomas Wintour which was signed Thomas Winter — obviously the confession had been altered if not invented completely to make it politically convenient. To make this story suitable for the stage, it was not possible to include everything, especially the full details of the church's involvement in the plot (much of which is subject to speculation anyway), and some of the minor characters have had to be altered or even omitted.

The single biggest mystery of the story regards the warning note; to this day nobody knows who sent it, and there is even a suggestion that there never was a note at all and that Mounteagle was yet another of Cecil's puppets. Happily such concerns can be left to academics; I've just tried to present the facts as I found them, and hope that others find them as fascinating as I did.

Kjartan Poskitt

MUSICAL NUMBERS

ACT I

1 **Cabaret Time** — All
2 The intro to "Smile As You Go"
3 The intro for "Cabaret Time"
4 "He's A Man" intro only
5 **He's A Man** — All
6 The intro to "Something in the Cupboard"
7 **Something in the Cupboard** — King James and Chorus
8 "The Quiet Guy" intro
9 "The Quiet Guy" intro
10 **The Quiet Guy** — Catesby and the Conspirators
11 **Nothing!** — Dorothy, Catherine Wheel and Chorus
12 **Thirty-Six Barrels** — Conspirators and Chorus
13 Reprise a few last chords of "Thirty-Six Barrels"

ACT II

14 **One Hell of a Guy** — Cecil, Eunice, Matthew and Chorus
15 An instrumental piece of "Nothing!"
16 **The Girl That Never Was** — Dorothy, Family and Chorus
17 The intro music "One Hell of a Guy"
18 Brief drum roll as Waad pulls the cloth away. As the equipment is revealed we hear some of the intro music from "Hell of a Guy"
19 **Fawkes Talks** — All
20 **A Thousand Angry Men** (verse 1) — Conspirators
21 **A Thousand Angry Men** (verse 2) — Conspirators
22 **A Thousand Angry Men** (verse 3) — Conspirators
23 **A Thousand Angry Men** (verse 4) — Conspirators
24 "The Quiet Guy"
25 **Smile As You Go** — Mrs Fawkes, Mrs Percy, Mrs Wright, Conspirators and Chorus
26 **Cabaret Finale** — Catherine Wheel and All

The full piano/vocal score is available from Samuel French Ltd.

A tape of backing tracks for all the songs and other music cues listed in the text is available for use in productions, as are additional band parts (for bass, drums, guitar, trumpet, trombone and sax/clarinet) to go with the piano/vocal score. These may be obtained by separate arrangement with the author who may be contacted via Samuel French Ltd.

A demonstration tape of all the main songs is available on free loan so you can hear the music before committing yourself to a production. All tracks were written and recorded by Kjartan Poskitt with additional vocals by Carol Turner and Juliet Waters.

ACKNOWLEDGEMENTS

I'd like to thank my wife Bridget for loyally supporting all my shows and saying "that was super" afterwards, and for making our daughters Maisie and Florence understand that they have to do the same. I'd also like to especially thank my best chum Richard Jennings who has been saying "that was super" for over twenty years, even when it sometimes wasn't.

Kjartan Poskitt

Musicals by the same author published by
Samuel French Ltd:
Henry the Tudor Dude
The Rumpelstiltskin Racket
Sammy's Magic Garden

ACT I

Scene 1

The Cabaret Club

The scene is the stage of "Catesby's" night-club. There is a "Catesby's" sign which is lit. To the side is a trick table (which is covered in a long cloth) and possibly other tables and chairs

The stage has not been cleaned since the previous night which was obviously rather a rough occasion. There are one or two broken chairs, the odd abandoned piece of clothing, and possibly a sword embedded in the back wall. Half of a manky-looking pie is on the floor

As the House Lights go off, two doorpersons arrive on stage. One of them, Eunice (a very big tough sort), prepares the stage area by clearing the mess away and lighting a few lanterns. The other, Matthew, addresses the audience

Matthew All right, ladies and gentlemen, can we keep it down a minute. Before we start these are the house rules. One, there is to be no kissing of the wenches while they are singing and dancing. Two, no fighting or violence until after the show is over. Three, all sheep, pigs and cattle to be left outside. Four, no discharging of foodstuffs or anything else from the mouth. Five… (*He picks up the pie from the floor and holds it gingerly*) No throwing things.

Eunice sees the pie, takes it and bites into it

Anybody who breaks these rules ——

Eunice — we take them round the office.

So saying, Eunice squishes the rest of the pie in Matthew's hand as a threat

Matthew Got that? OK, let it roll.

Matthew and Eunice go off

1: Cabaret Time

As the introduction plays, the lively chorus all charge up to the stage through the auditorium, and generally shout greetings at people in the audience such as "Hallo Butch!" "You here again?" "I see you left the old man at home tonight." "Sorry I missed you Tuesday." "Have you had your operation yet?" etc. They then assemble and sing

Chorus It's cabaret time down at Catesby's
We hope you get a laugh and a thrill
It's one of those shows
Where anything goes
And before we close it probably will.

You'll have a fabaret time down at Catesby's
We're gonna see you're all right
You can depend
Before it's the end
All your little worries will be well on the mend
It's hallo stranger goodbye old friend
At Catesby's cabaret
Tonight.

The music drops for an announcement

Matthew Ladies and gentlemen, will you please welcome the girl who put the spin into spinster — your hostess Miss Catherine Wheel...

Catherine Wheel enters

The chorus lead the applause. Catherine speaks to the audience over the instrumental second verse — if necessary alter her dialogue to fit

Catherine Wheel Evening everybody, how are you? All expecting a night of genteel sophistication no doubt. Look, we've even got fresh sawdust on the floor. Mind you, that was last night's furniture. So let's start as we mean to go on, how many Catholics have we got in?

There is a cheer from the chorus

Dare I ask, any Protestants? Scottish Presbyterian? Greek Orthodox? Harbour orthodox?

Some voices from the chorus shout "Harbour orthodox"?

That's where our Maggie goes when she's praying for sailors. Harbour or the docks. Anyway whoever you are, your money's always welcome. Hey, do you know what this lot are? Puritans! That's right, Puritans.

The chorus adopt angelic poses pretending to be Puritans

Listen. Hey, do you lot like singing?
Chorus (*chanting*) No we do not like singing.
Catherine Wheel Do you like dancing?
Chorus (*chanting*) No we do not like dancing.
Catherine Wheel That's just as well because they can't do either. Watch!

The chorus do a dance for the third verse

Very fancy! Be honest, have you lot been practising?
Chorus Yes.
Catherine Wheel All right, we'll believe you.

Moll gets an undergarment twisted and is adjusting it

Come on Moll, when you're ready we've got the last verse to do. Comfy now? Good, let's wrap it up then…

All (*singing*)
It's cabaret time down at Catesby's
Kick off your shoes and relax
You'll even find
It slips from your mind
If you're behind in paying your tax.

You'll have a fabaret time down at Catesby's
So fasten your seats for the flight
You know what they say
Be happy today
The sorrows of tomorrow are a lifetime away
It's fun fun fun fun fun all the way
At Catesby's cabaret
Tonight!

All cheer. Some chorus members go to sit at the tables

The rest of the chorus go off leaving Catherine Wheel to address the audience

Catherine Wheel Before we go on, what do you think of the seventeenth century so far? We're only three years in and we've already got a dead queen. And tell me, have you all been to church this week? Confusing isn't it? Just a few months ago here in England, our old English Elizabeth wanted us all to be Church of England. Catholics might not have liked it, but at least it was straightforward. Now we've got a Scottish King who's Presbyterian, but his wife's Danish, his mum's Catholic, and do you know who his father was? No? Well you're not alone, even his mum wasn't too sure! What's worse, when they first made him King of Scotland, do you know what he said?

Someone dressed as a baby wearing a crown with a nappy and a rattle comes on

Baby Waahhh!

Suddenly there is a commotion

Some armed Puritans headed by Oliver rush on

The gang all stay very close together glancing around anxiously

Oliver Nobody move!
Catherine Wheel I hope you've got tickets.
Oliver We have reason to believe this place belongs to the Catholic Robert Catesby.
Moll He saw the sign!
Beth You mean the big sign with lights all round it?
Maggie Who's a clever boy then?
Oliver I'm warning you, this freak show is against the law.
Catherine Wheel Rubbish. We have to go to the Protty church on Sundays or pay a fine. The rest of the week's our business, there's no law.
Oliver There is God's law.
Beth Oh yeah, the eleventh commandment ——
Moll "Thou shalt not wear a fancy frock and tell jokes."
Oliver Enough. We seek out Jesuits.
Catherine Wheel Jesuits?
Oliver Catholics with attitude. They creep over from France and Spain, to stir up the embers of revolution.

Catherine Wheel Well goodness gracious.
Oliver Men, search this rat hole.
Maggie The tall one can come and search me.
Jenny Huh! You'd have to tell him what to look for.

The other girls all start taunting the Puritans shouting things like: "Hey, I'm a Jesuit. Come and search me!" "Me too. How about it?" etc.

As the girls advance on the terrified Puritans, Catherine and Jenny go to sit at the trick table. The Baby comes and stands beside them. The girls are accosting Oliver

Moll Hey, what's the difference between a Puritan and a mushroom?
Maggie You can call a mushroom a "fun-guy".
Beth I've got a better one. How many Puritans does it take to light a candle?
Girls None!
Beth They don't need to light candles because they all think the sun shines out of their ——
Oliver Silence!

Jenny pulls the rear of the Baby's nappy outwards and looks down it

Jenny Oh look! I've found a Jesuit.

The Puritans all rush towards her

Sorry, my mistake. (*She sniffs*) It's a little Puritan.
Baby Get your filthy hands out.
Catherine Wheel So how many have you found then?
Oliver We'll be back.
Maggie Don't forget to bring the tall one. Night-night, darling!

The chorus all whistle loudly as:

The Puritans go off

Catherine Wheel Go on girls, the fun's over. Some customers still have money so mingle mingle mingle.

Catesby enters

Beth It's Sir Robin!

The girls all cluster round him

Catesby Easy girls! I'm a married man.
Maggie That's just a nasty rumour that your wife started.
Catesby Get off, and behave yourselves.

All remaining chorus and the Baby go off

Catesby goes to where Catherine is sitting

I hear the Puritans came knocking.
Catherine Wheel Ah, but they didn't knock in the right place did they? Out you come, Father.

Catherine knocks on the trick table

Father Henry Garnet comes from underneath

Catesby Henry! I thought you were in France.
Garnet So I sneak about a bit, don't I?
Catesby Well your sneaking days are nearly over. The Catholic bashers are on their way out.
Garnet You think so?
Catherine Wheel Stands to reason. First we had Henry the Eighth ——
Catesby Catholic basher.
Catherine Wheel — then Bloody Mary ——
Catesby Protestant basher.
Garnet Good girl.
Catherine Wheel — then Elizabeth the Virgin ——
Catesby Catholic basher.
Catherine Wheel — and now we've got Jim the Jock.
Catesby He's got to be a Prot basher if he's half a man.
Catherine Wheel Half a man, eh? Funny you should say that.
Catesby Why?
Catherine Wheel There's a little ditty going round:

His tongue's too big for his head
His wife's too small for his bed
So if he dribbles when he talks
And he wiggles when he walks
King Jim — that's him.

Catesby Catherine, do me a favour. If he comes in here, zip your lip.
Catherine Wheel You know me, Robin. Ever the professional.

Catherine exits

Catesby All this hiding under tables, you must find it highly grieving.
Garnet Highly grieving indeed.
Catesby Never mind, we'll soon have this Scottish King sorted. If he doesn't grieve us, we won't grieve him, know what I mean, Henry?
Garnet Got it in one, my son.

The Lights fade to Black-out. The Catesby's sign goes off

Garnet and Catesby exit

Music 2. The intro music to "Smile As You Go" covers the change to the next scene

Scene 2

Mrs Fawkes' living-room

The Lights come up on Mrs Fawkes who is being visited by Mrs Percy and the stony-faced Mrs Wright

Mrs Fawkes (*shouting off*) Guy? *Guy*! Mrs Percy and Mrs Wright are here. Are you coming to say hallo or what? *Guy*?
Mrs Percy They're all the same, Edith.
Mrs Fawkes Mine is. Ever since he got back from Spain.
Mrs Percy Spain?
Mrs Fawkes Doing a bit of fighting.
Mrs Percy Very sensible. Fighting keeps 'em out of trouble, eh Doris?
Mrs Wright I'm saying nothing.
Mrs Percy By the way, did you give any more thought to going Catholic?
Mrs Fawkes Already gone.
Mrs Percy Fancy! You never said.
Mrs Fawkes My last husband got us in.
Mrs Percy So now you're Hail Mary-ing?
Mrs Fawkes And genuflecting ——
Mrs Percy — and confessing?
Mrs Fawkes Oh yes, definitely confessing, aren't I Doris?
Mrs Wright I'm saying nothing.

They have a good dirty chuckle

Mrs Fawkes *Guy*, are you coming in here?
Mrs Percy He doesn't have to.

Mrs Fawkes He does. I'll get him.

Mrs Fawkes stomps off

(*Off*) Guido Fawkes, are you coming through now, or do I have to drag you? Well? OK you asked for it.

Mrs Fawkes returns pushing a chair. On it is a full-size, fully-clothed traditional Guy Fawkes dummy. Throughout the show, the dummy is spoken to and treated like a real human being

Say hallo, Guy.
Mrs Percy Hallo young Guy. You're looking well.
Mrs Fawkes Hallo? Guy?
Mrs Percy Anyone home?
Mrs Fawkes He spends all day like this, just moping round the house.
Mrs Percy I hate it when they mope.
Mrs Fawkes He's always moped.
Mrs Percy They're all the same, teenagers.
Mrs Fawkes Teenager? He's thirty-four years old! I wish he'd get out more.
Mrs Percy My Thomas'll take him out. He's calling by in a minute.
Mrs Fawkes Oh no, not that sweaty little creep?
Mrs Percy I'll have you know, he's Constable of Alnwick Castle now.
Mrs Fawkes Alnwick? Best place for him, eh Doris?
Mrs Wright I'm saying nothing.
Thomas Percy (*off*) Anybody home?
Mrs Percy That sounds like him. Brace yourselves.

Thomas Percy and John Wright enter

Thomas Percy Hallo, Mother. Here I am, your pride and joy. Look who I've found.
John Wright How do, Mother.
Thomas Percy Ooh Jack, I can see where you get your good looks from.
Mrs Wright
John Wright } (*together*) I'm saying nothing.
Mrs Fawkes Jack Wright! Weren't you at St Peter's School with my Guy?
John Wright In York? 'Appen I was.
Thomas Percy And I married his sister Martha. Small world, innit?
Mrs Percy And where is Martha exactly?
Thomas Percy How should I know? London somewhere.
Mrs Fawkes Fine way to treat a wife.

Thomas Percy Don't worry, I've got another one. Honestly, mothers! What are they like, eh?
Mrs Percy I thought you were off to Catesby's.
Mrs Fawkes Don't let us keep you.
Thomas Percy Hey Guy, you coming? We are in for one mental night.
Mrs Fawkes I don't want my Guy getting into any trouble.
Thomas Percy Is she still yakking? Come on, Guy, let's go.

Thomas Percy and John Wright pick up Fawkes between them and loop his arms over their shoulders just like three normal lads might do

Mrs Percy You'll keep a sensible eye on them, won't you, Jack?
John Wright Oh ay.
Thomas Percy Never mind us. You old girls behave yourselves or I'll have you burnt as witches.

Thomas Percy and John Wright exit with Fawkes

Mrs Fawkes Think they're so smart, don't they?
Mrs Percy Youth of today, what can you do?
Mrs Fawkes The trouble is, they know they can do what they want ——
Mrs Percy — and get away with it, like that kid last week ——
Mrs Fawkes — caught stealing a sheep ——
Mrs Percy —what did they do?
Mrs Fawkes
Mrs Percy } (*together*) Hung him.
Mrs Percy Dead in twenty minutes.
Mrs Fawkes What kind of deterrent is that?
Mrs Percy You know what they really want?
Mrs Fawkes
Mrs Percy } (*together*) *Drawing and quartering*!
Mrs Fawkes That's it, they want their inners cutting out ——
Mrs Percy — burning on a plate in front of them ——
Mrs Fawkes — make the smoke go right up their noses ——
Mrs Percy — best thing for them.
Mrs Fawkes Not much chance of re-offending after that, eh Doris?
Mrs Percy She's saying nothing.
Mrs Fawkes } (*together*) She's saying nothing.
Mrs Wright I'm saying nothing.

Music 3. The intro for "Cabaret Time" covers the change to the next scene

Scene 3

The Cabaret Club

The "Catesby's" sign comes on again. The music may continue quietly to underscore the start of the scene and add to the atmosphere

Matthew and Eunice stand by the door. Thomas Percy, John Wright and Guy Fawkes come in. They sit at a table, Guy slumps over. Thomas Percy is looking round

John Wright This'll do for us. What's up with 'ee?
Thomas Percy I can't see her. She said she'd be here.
John Wright Who?
Thomas Percy She's called Lily Gage and she's a bit classy actually.
John Wright This is a classy place an' all.
Thomas Percy You want to see the toilets — they've got separate buckets for ladies and gents.

A waitress with a bland smile approaches

Waitress Good-evening, welcome to Catesby's. My name is Denise and I'll be your waitress for this evening. We hope you enjoy your visit.
John Wright What's there to drink, please?
Waitress We have a full range of refreshing cocktails including the Roman Candle, the Jumping Jack, the Silver Rain, the Volcano, the Banshee Whistler and tonight's special is the Rocket Surprise.
John Wright Rocket Surprise? What's that about?
Waitress It sends you over the moon and you end up seeing stars, sir.
John Wright Three of them then, please.
Waitress Thank you, sir. (*She turns to go*)
John Wright Hang on, miss! These two haven't ordered yet.

Catherine Wheel comes on to the stage. (*This could be heralded by a little drum roll*)

Catherine Wheel Ladies and gents, it's my delight to tell you that we have a very special guest with us tonight. Will you please slip the latch, pull the handle and let it out for the handsome smashing Spanish bashing Sir Walter Raleigh.

Everyone cheers as Raleigh comes on

Raleigh Thank you, thank you, really you shouldn't … it's nothing.
Catherine Wheel Now then, Sir Walter, you've just been to the New World, what have you brought back this time?
Raleigh I bring the potato and tobacco.
Catherine Wheel So what do we do with the potato then?
Raleigh First you chip it into shape.
Catherine Wheel And what's that shape called?
Raleigh I call it — the chip!
Catherine Wheel Then what do you do?
Raleigh You put it in your mouth like so.

Raleigh holds a chip as if holding a cigarette. He pretends to puff on it and so on

Catherine Wheel Do you think it'll catch on, Wally?
Raleigh Oh yes. People will be buying packets, maybe getting through twenty a day. They'll be saying "I've tried to give up but I can't."
Catherine Wheel And what do we do with tobacco then?
Raleigh You fry it and eat it with fish.
Catherine Wheel Ladies and gentlemen, let's hear it for big Wally!

All cheer

Raleigh Thank you, thank you.
Catherine Wheel Sir Walter, with your permission we've been practising a little tribute to you.
Raleigh Really? I say, that's awfully awfully, you know.

Music 4. The "He's A Man" intro starts

Chorus (*singing*) Sir Walter Raleigh, Sir Walter Raleigh,
Sir Walter Ra Ra Ra Ra
Raleigh, Raleigh, Raleigh, Raleigh
Raleigh, Raleigh *etc.*

But Catesby dashes on

Catesby Hold it! He's here.

The music stops

Catherine Wheel Who?
Catesby The King.

Maggie Oh no. I haven't shaved my legs for weeks.
Catesby Don't do any songs likely to offend him.
Catherine Wheel But that's all of them.

We hear massive cheering outside

King James's rather precious Groom of the Bedchamber enters and glances round then shouts off

Groom It looks safe enough. Tatty but safe.

King James nervously dashes in, glancing nervously back through the door

King James What is that rabble? And why is that rabble rabbling?
Groom They just want to see their new King, what with you in your smart new crown and everything.
King James *Guards*! Send them away!
Groom Oh go on with you, they're only after a look at your face.
King James (*shouting*) Why don't I pull my breeches down and they can look upon my backside?

Absolute sudden silence. Everyone gawps at James. The Groom chuckles

Catesby (*whispering*) That's him?
King James Where is my advisor? Hurry, you sad pollop.
Groom Sad pollop he says! Hasn't himself got some tongue today!

The sinister Robert Cecil enters. He instructs Matthew and Eunice

Cecil You two, watch this door. His Majesty wishes to rest.
Catesby (*aghast*) No! It's Robert Cecil!

Cecil sees the sign

Cecil Catesby? That name is familiar.
Catherine Wheel Go, Robin! Disappear.

Catesby hides under the trick table

King James What place is this?
Cecil (*to Matthew*) You. Speak.
Matthew It's just a little club.

King James A club! May we join?
Catherine Wheel Of course. A seat for the King, boys. Move it!

Thomas Percy and John Wright jump away from their table, leaving Guy slumped over

King James Thank you both kindly. My Groom of the Bedchamber shall sit with me.
Groom (*seeing Catherine*) Do I love that frock!

Catherine gives the Groom a funny look as he and King James sit at their seats. Cecil has nowhere to sit. He shouts at Guy

Cecil Move boy!
King James Shhh, Sir Robert. This fellow sleeps.
Cecil But I do not have a seat.
King James So? I will not have him disturbed. This sleeping fellow can do me no harm.

The waitress brings a fancy looking glassful over, then waits to one side

Waitress House special with the manager's compliments, sir.

Everybody stares as James drinks and dribbles

Maggie Are you sure that's the King?

James burps

Catherine Wheel That's him.
Cecil Sire, I remember: Catesby is a Catholic name!
King James So? Do Catholics not worship God like other men?
Cecil In their own foul way.
King James And I, the King, am I not divine?
Cecil Yes.
King James So they do also worship me, yes?

Thomas Percy does a big bow

Thomas Percy Please, Your Majestic Highness.
Groom He spreads it thick, doesn't he?
King James I can take it. So who is this?

Thomas Percy Thomas Percy, a Catholic who welcomes you, sire. Indeed all Catholics welcome you, sire, as one of us, because was not your own mother a Catholic?

King James My own mother did not see me after my first year.

Cecil See? That is how the King was treated by a Catholic, his own mother too. No wonder he is like he is.

King James What am I like Sir Robert? (*He drinks and dribbles again*)

Groom Yes, you tell him, Sir Robert. What's he like?

Cecil You favour the Protestant cause, sire.

King James Sir Robert, do you forget I was kidnapped by Protestants in my sixteenth year? Maybe I am not disposed to either.

Thomas Percy But I understand your Queen has become Catholic, sire.

King James Our Annie is first and foremost my loyal and lovely wife.

Thomas Percy Sire, all Catholics will be loyal and lovely to you, all we ask is just a little tolerance.

King James Thank you, Thomas Percy. You have my assurance I will not persecute any that will be quiet and give an outward obedience to the law.

John Wright I'll drink to that.

General agreement

Cecil But, sire ——

King James And Sir Robert, I will not refuse to promote any of them whose good service deserves it.

John Wright I'll drink to that an' all.

There is a general cheer from the crowd which makes James very nervy

King James Why does everybody have to shout at me?

Groom There there, it's only a bit of cheering.

King James Is there no music instead?

Catherine Wheel Oh — we don't know any.

Groom Now there's a whopper. You were playing when we came in.

Catherine Wheel It wasn't very good.

Cecil Play!

5: He's a Man

This song has several lines that can be sung as solos by different people

Chorus

Sir Walter Ra — leigh
Sir Walter Ra — leigh
Sir Walter Ra — Ra — Ra — Ra —

Raleigh Raleigh Raleigh Raleigh
Raleigh Raleigh Raleigh Raleigh
Raleigh Raleigh Raleigh Ra

Solo He's marvellous and mighty, he's a man
All *He's a man*!
Solo He never ducks a fight
All 'Cos he's a man
He's a diamond he's a pearl
He's the dream of every girl
'Cos he's a man, yes he's a man!

Solo He's the hunky heart of Devon, he's a man
All *He's a man*!
Solo He's a little chunk of heaven
All He's a man
He's a poet and a scholar
In a ruffled lacy collar
He's a man he's a man he's a man.

Our hearts are ailing when he's sailing
On the seven seas
Our tears all flow each time he goes away
Does he hear our voices whisper on the ocean breeze?
It's him we sigh for, him we cry for
Every single day.

He smashes up the Spanish, he's a man
He's a man!
And he makes Armadas vanish
He's a man
He's sailed the Spanish Main
Where he smashed them once again
'Cos he's a man, yes he's a man!

He sailed the Irish sea 'cos he's a man
He's a man
Brought the Irish to their knees
'Cos he's a man
The Queen was so delighted
That she had Sir Walter knighted
He's a man he's a man he's a man!

Our hearts are ailing when he's sailing
On the seven seas
Our tears all flow each time he goes away
Does he hear our voices whisper on the ocean breeze?
It's him we sigh for, him we cry for
Every single day.

He raids the Caribbean, he's a man
He's a man!
He's an anti-European he's a man
With his land and his riches
He's the butchest thing in britches

He's a man, he's a man
He's an R-A-L-E-I-G-H
He's a really really really really
Raleigh Raleigh Raleigh real man.
A real man!

There is a big cheer

Catherine Wheel and the chorus girls can go off

King James And exactly what was that about?
Groom Sir Walter Raleigh. He's marvellous and mighty and he never wears a nightie, he's a man…
King James And is that what "men" do? Attack Spain?
Raleigh Absolutely, it's great fun.
King James Well I want peace with Spain. Arrest him.
Raleigh Gosh.
King James And execute him.
John Wright You what? With no trial?
King James I am the King. My word is life and death.
John Wright Oi! King or not, thy better learn't' rules down here and fast.
Groom Come on, sire, he's a bit big for us.

The Groom hurriedly ushers King James off——

Matthew and Eunice manage to restrain John Wright. Cecil remains and stares at John Wright

Matthew Leave it.
Eunice It's not worth it!

Cecil So, you would threaten your monarch?
John Wright And who art thee, weirdo?
Cecil Look at my face very carefully. I am your worst nightmare, Catholic.

Matthew and Eunice release John Wright

You two, bring Raleigh.

Matthew and Eunice glance at each other

From now on you work for me.

Matthew and Eunice decide it's best to do as they are told. They gingerly hold Raleigh who consoles them

Raleigh Don't look so worried, chaps. I hear he pays good wages.
Cecil Let's get out of this cesspit.

Matthew and Eunice lead Raleigh away

John Wright He'll never execute Raleigh. He 'ant got the bottle.
Cecil And what will you do? Remember, you little Catholics have all promised to be good little boys.

Cecil goes off

Waitress Have a nice day now.

Catesby and Garnet come out from under the trick table

Catesby You blithering fools.
Garnet Bang out of order.
Catesby Why can't you behave like your friend here? Haven't we got problems enough without you winding them up?
John Wright But he took Sir Walter.
Catesby So what? Walter can look out for himself. Who's going to look out for us if Cecil turns the King against Catholics?
Thomas Percy Cecil's a weirdo.
Catesby You wouldn't say that to his face.
John Wright I just did.
Garnet Blinkin' Nora!
Catesby You better shut up. And sit down.

Wright and Percy nervously rejoin Fawkes. Catesby looks furious

Denise, over here.

The waitress runs up

Waitress Yes, sir?
Catesby Remember these faces. If ever they try and come in here again — give them the best table and whatever they want for their dinner.

Catesby sits with them chuckling and Garnet joins them

So you called Cecil a weirdo, did you? We've got a lot to talk about.

Maggie comes in shepherding Mounteagle by the arm. Jenny, Moll, Beth and maybe others come on from another direction. During the following, Dorothy comes on separately

Maggie Jenny, look what just sailed in.
Jenny Hallo darlin'! Want your fortune told?
Moll I bet you've got a strong love line!
Mounteagle Ladies please, have you seen the King?
Maggie Yeah, but don't worry.
Beth He's not a patch on you.
Dorothy Billy?
Mounteagle Dorothy!
Jenny Hands off, new girl.
Maggie We saw him first.

Mounteagle politely disengages himself from the girls

Mounteagle Sorry ladies, but Dorothy and I used to play together.
Moll Lucky cow.
Dorothy This is Lord Mounteagle, everybody.
Chorus Hallo, big boy!
Mounteagle I haven't seen you for years.
Dorothy Three years, two months, one week and four days actually.
Mounteagle You counted?
Dorothy Oh — not really. Just a guess.
Mounteagle Just look at you! I wondered where you'd got to.
Dorothy Well, here I am, in a show, seeing the world, all pretty boring really. But what brings you here?
Mounteagle I'm supposed to be part of the Royal retinue.

Jenny Are you?
Maggie Is he?
Mounteagle I've just started. The King picked me especially.
Jenny I bet he did.
Beth What a waste.

The girls (except Dorothy) suddenly lose interest. Mounteagle sees the sign

Mounteagle Catesby's? Does that mean Sir Robert Catesby?
Dorothy Er, not necessarily.

Mounteagle spots Catesby who is very uncomfortable at being recognized

Mounteagle In fact, isn't that him? Robin?
Catesby I'm only Robin to my friends.
Mounteagle But our families were always friends.
Catesby Catholic friends.
Mounteagle Of course.
Catesby And working for the King, are you still a Catholic?
Mounteagle Well, you know — sort of. It's just this job was going with the new King and in the interview they mentioned religion and I sort of said C of E, but it was just a formality. He's all right old James, I don't think he really minds whether you're Anglican Church or Definitely Catholic.
Catesby Anglican Church or Definitely Catholic?
Mounteagle Yes, or as he says ACDC. I say, isn't that Father Henry?
Garnet Who?
Mounteagle Father Henry Garnet! Still a Jesuit, Henry?
Garnet You've got the wrong bloke.
Mounteagle Oh come on Henry, of course it's you.
Garnet Tell him to knock it on the head.
Catesby He doesn't know you.
Garnet I'm just a geezer, right?
Mounteagle But Henry…
Catesby You never seen him.

Catesby and Garnet shuffle away, Catesby indicating to John Wright, Thomas Percy and Fawkes that they should follow

As they all go, the girls sit to one side minding their own business

Mounteagle Oh gosh. It seems no-one wants to know me these days.
Dorothy Oh Bill, I do. It's so brilliant they made you a lord.
Mounteagle They should have made you a lady.

Dorothy Do you think so?
Mounteagle Definitely. Are you all right?
Dorothy I was just thinking — but it's silly.
Mounteagle Go on. Tell me. Forget the lord bit, I'm still Billy.
Dorothy Well, if you're a lord, you could make me a lady.
Mounteagle How?
Dorothy Lady Mounteagle.
Mounteagle Oh what a sweet idea; but Dorothy, there already is a Lady Mounteagle.
Dorothy You're married?
Mounteagle Of course. You'll meet her one day, you're sure to get on.
Dorothy Oh sure.
Mounteagle Dorothy?
Dorothy The King went ages ago, you better get off. You don't want to get into trouble.
Mounteagle Are you all right?
Dorothy Fine. Why shouldn't I be? It was great to see you again, Bill.
Mounteagle You too, Dorothy. Maybe I'll see you again in another three years two months — whatever it was.
Dorothy One week four days. Bye then, Bill.
Mounteagle Goodbye, Dorothy. You look great.

Mounteagle goes off

Jenny Wasting your time there.
Maggie He's a King's man.
Dorothy I know what you're getting at, but you're wrong. If you must know, he has a wife, so there.
Moll So does the King.
Beth "Our Annie."
Maggie And he has four kids.
Jenny God knows how.
Dorothy Oh shut up.
Girls Wooo!

Catherine Wheel enters

Catherine Wheel Come on, less lip and more zip or you'll be late for the dream sequence.

The Lights fade

Music 6. The intro to "Something in the Cupboard" plays as the scene is set for:

Scene 4

King James's Bedroom

The only necessary props are a cupboard in the corner, and a bed with sheets, pillows and blankets

The Lights come up and we find King James in bed. Cecil has obviously been summoned to see him for a late-night tantrum

King James I hate him, I hate him, I hate him, I hate him. Hate hate hate.
Cecil Can't this wait till morning, sire?
King James Why should it? *I hate him.*
Cecil But you can't execute Sir Walter Raleigh just like that.
King James You arrogant little squitter, don't you ever tell me what I can't do. I hung that cutpurse at Newark "just like that", didn't I? Pulled him out of the crowd and strung him straight up.
Cecil But Sir Walter is a national hero.
King James So? I'm a national hero. Ask anyone in Newark, they thought I was dead hard.
Cecil Sire, Sir Walter Raleigh is rather more than a common thief. There will have to be a trial first.
King James A trial, you gumboil? And exactly what are we supposed to charge him with?
Cecil Let's say he's plotting with the Spanish to put Arabella Stuart on your throne.
King James He's plotting with the Spanish? There, what did I tell you, he's out to get me.
Cecil Sire, do try and pay attention. Raleigh isn't really plotting with the Spanish, he attacks them!
King James He attacks them? But I want peace with Spain. At this rate they'll send another Armada. They're out to get me too, you know.
Cecil There there, sire, the Spanish will never get you.
King James Really?
Cecil Really, sire, I promise. Now go to sleep.

James is placated. He turns over to sleep. Cecil starts to enjoy himself

If anything, the French will get you first.
King James *What*?

Cecil It's tradition. The French have always hated the English.
King James But I'm Scottish.
Cecil Oh of course you are. Sorry, sire, I forgot. Good-night then, and don't worry, sire, you'll be fine.
King James Yes. Of course I will.

James turns over to sleep again

Cecil Just as long as the English don't come for you.
King James *What*? But I'm the King!
Cecil Yes, but you're still a bit of a Jock, aren't you? Only the other day you told Parliament you were going to scrap the name "England". That was a bit classic, even by your standards, sire.
King James Surely they can't all hate me.
Cecil Of course not, sire. They love you.
King James Do they? Oh good, Sir Robert, do they really?
Cecil Oh yes, sire. They all love you.

James turns over again

Except — the Catholics.
James *Arghh*!

James buries himself in fear under the bedclothes

Cecil smugly saunters off

7: Something in the Cupboard

The musical introduction starts

Catherine Wheel enters

James is unaware of her

During her speech the chorus members come and prepare for the song. They could bring on other props as needed such as curtains, a chair, a teddy and so on

Catherine Wheel Ladies and gentlemen, if you'll forgive a slightly personal question, how well do you sleep at night? Maybe you're one of the lucky ones, and if so, we now invite you to spare a thought for those among us who aren't quite so fortunate.

Chorus (*singing*) The sunset dims to let the night descend
Another weary day is drawing to the end
So bend your knees and
Close your eyes up tight
And say a little prayer to get you through the night…

During the following verse, James nervously creeps round doing appropriate actions. He treats everything the chorus sings as though he is talking to himself

You check behind the curtains
And you see there's nothing there
You look beneath the bed
And even underneath the chair
You pull out all the pillows
And you reach along behind
There's nothing there to get you
'Cos it's only in your mind.

James nods. Chorus members help him into bed, tuck him in and pass his teddy

So roll back all the blankets
And straighten out the sheet
Have a little stretch and
Let the weight come off your feet
Tuck up all your tootsie toes
And cuddle up to Ted.
And just ignore the little voice
That whispers in your head that …

The cupboard starts rocking and banging!

There's something in the cupboard
And it wants to get out
King James I can hear it scratching
And a-moving about
Chorus Your tummy is a-tremble
And your knees they both shake
King James While it's there
I'm staying well awake.

Suggestion: in the next verse King James takes his teddy to the cupboard. When he opens the door, he makes the teddy look inside first, then peers round himself afterwards. Of course the inside of the cupboard holds no nasty surprises

Chorus You know you're going crazy
But you must be really sure
You take a massive breath
And then you reach towards the door
But everything is normal
And there's nothing out of place
So you try to get a grip
And put a smile upon your face

You climb back into bed
As if you hadn't got a care,
But are you really certain
That there wasn't something there?
Your spine is all a-shiver
And your head is in a sweat
'Cos it's time to blow your candle out——

King James *No*! *Not yet* because ——

The cupboard starts rocking and banging again

Chorus There's something in the cupboard
And it wants to get out
You can hear it scratching
And a-moving about

Your tummy is a-tremble
And your knees they both shake

King James While it's there
I'm staying well awake.

Chorus members open the cupboard doors, and again show it to be normal. They shut the doors

During this last verse, the chorus drift off to leave King James alone

Chorus Drink some milk or maybe count some sheep
The more you wake the worse it is to sleep
You're on your own, it's up to you
What are you going to do?

He suddenly jumps out of bed and strides towards the cupboard

King James (*spoken*) On my mother's grave! This is ridiculous.

He pulls open the cupboard doors and the Fawkes dummy springs out at him. He screams! (see "Staging Suggestions" p.78)

Big chord. Black-out

SCENE 5

The Cabaret Club

The "Catesby's" sign is on

John Wright, Thomas Percy and Fawkes sit at the trick table

Catesby comes in ranting to Thomas Wintour

Catesby I don't believe it. He's let that leech Cecil get to him. He hasn't got the nerve to wipe his own backside without asking Sir Bloody Robert Cecil first.
Thomas Percy Good-evening, Sir Robin.
Catesby What? Oh yeah, hallo boys. This is Thomas Wintour, the bloke I told you about. Catholic heart, lawyer's brain, a very handy mover.
John Wright How do.
Catesby Right, we've got to do something to stop the Catholics going belly up. And we have to do it now.
Thomas Percy Is it that bad? After all, the King did promise tolerance.
Catesby Of course it's that bad. Look!

Catesby bangs on the trick table

Father Henry Garnet comes out

How come we've still got a priest living under the table? It's bad, isn't it, Father?

Garnet Well bad.
Catesby Henry here has been sounding out people in Rome for us.
Thomas Wintour What people?
Garnet Big people.
Catesby Big unhappy people. People who want Catholic tolerance in England.
Thomas Wintour But we'd have to change the whole government.
Garnet Big people do big things.
Catesby So if we had to do something big ——
Garnet — the man from Roma, he says yes.
Catesby Thanks, Henry. Off you go, and watch out for the coastguard.

Garnet quickly disguises himself. (*He could whip off his black robes to reveal shorts, Hawaiian shirt and sandals underneath. He then dons some dark glasses and a silly hat, and shoves the robes in a bag covered in travel labels*)

Garnet swiftly leaves

Thomas Percy Where's he going?
Catesby Away. Henry doesn't need to know any more and Henry doesn't want to know any more. Henry's done his bit, he's got us Rome's approval.
Thomas Wintour Approval to do what?
Catesby Now that's an interesting question.
John Wright What about kidnapping Cecil?
Percy How about asking the Archbishop of Canterbury to resign?
Catesby How about digging a tunnel under Parliament, stuffing the thing full of gunpowder and blowing the King, Cecil and the whole stinking lot of them to kingdom come?

The others all laugh briefly, dismissing this suggestion

Thomas Wintour How about printing a new Latin prayer book?
Thomas Percy How about getting a tax put on Protestant services?
Catesby I said: how about digging a tunnel under Parliament, stuffing the thing full of gunpowder and blowing the King, Cecil and the whole stinking lot of them to kingdom come?

The others laugh again briefly

Thomas Wintour How about getting the Pope to come and do a national tour?
John Wright No, I reckon we grab Cecil, and give him a right good thump.
Catesby Boys, I don't think you heard me. I said: how about digging a tunnel

under Parliament, stuffing the thing full of gunpowder and blowing the King, Cecil and the whole stinking lot of them to kingdom come?

This time they all turn to look at him aghast

The Lights fade to Black-out

They all go off in the Black-out

The Lights fade up again

Maggie and Jenny come on chatting

Maggie — so he said, "I hate carrying on behind my wife's back", and so I said, "Let her turn round and watch then, I don't care."

The girls shriek with laughter

Dorothy enters

Hallo, it's droopy Dorothy.
Jenny Missing your boyfriend, dearie?
Dorothy I don't have a boyfriend.
Jenny You better give her one of yours, Maggie. How about Bertie?
Maggie So what am I supposed to do Tuesday nights?
Jenny Arthur.
Maggie Not likely. I promoted him, he's Sunday mornings now.

Catherine Wheel enters

Catherine Wheel What are you two catting on about?
Jenny She's pining for that Lord Mounteagle.
Dorothy I'm not.
Catherine Wheel I hope you mean that. It's dangerous being in government. You'd be very hurt if something happened to him.
Dorothy Like what?
Jenny Do you know something, Catherine?
Catherine Wheel Yes. I know it's best to keep my mouth shut.
Jenny
Maggie } (*together*) Oh!
Maggie Look, it's Sir Robin!

Catesby enters

Jenny and Maggie hurry over to him

Jenny Where have you been?
Maggie You missed Christmas.
Jenny What have you done to your hands?
Catesby Nothing.
Catherine Wheel On your way, girls. Go and find some men to frighten.
Jenny But we haven't seen him for weeks!
Catherine Wheel Now!

Jenny and Maggie moan as they leave dragging Dorothy off

Catherine examines Catesby's hand

So, Robin — blisters, filthy fingernails, anybody might think you'd been digging.
Catesby No.
Catherine Wheel And you've rented a house from John Whynniard.
Catesby Who's he?
Catherine Wheel He did costumes for a show I did once.
Catesby So?
Catherine Wheel So now he's official Keeper of the Lords Wardrobe, and he owns a house just round the corner from the Lords Chamber.
Catesby Never heard of him.
Catherine Wheel Funny. I saw him the other day, and he's heard of you.
Catesby *What*?
Catherine Wheel Relax! I got it out of him, but nobody else will. So, you've got a house near the Lords and you've been digging a tunnel.
Catesby Tunnel! What do you know about a tunnel?
Catherine Wheel Apart from the state of your hands, you've got dirt all stuck in the back of your jacket, your knees and elbows are worn ——
Catesby Stop fussing, Catherine.
Catherine Wheel They say the foundations at Parliament are three yards thick. No wonder you've been busy.
Catesby If you breathe a word of this …
Catherine Wheel Never me, Robin, but I wish you'd take more care. If I know then maybe others can work it out. I tell you something else, I called by your house in Lambeth the other day. There was a Mr Keyes there.
Catesby Misery Keyes? What about him?
Catherine Wheel He's a rotten liar. I saw a pile of barrels in the back.
Catesby Wine. For the club, special import.
Catherine Wheel That's what he said. Funny that, because those barrels

were stamped with the armoury crest from the Tower of London. Do you know what barrels from the Tower normally contain? Not wine but ——

Thomas Percy, John Wright, and Thomas Wintour dash in

Thomas Percy Sir Robin, brilliant news!
John Wright Forget yon tunnel.
Thomas Percy We heard a cellar being cleared…
Catesby Shhh!
Catherine Wheel Well, I must be going. I'm sure you boys all have lots to talk about.

The gang all mutter goodbye as Catherine moves to exit

Catesby (*as she goes*) You dumb geeks!

Catherine exits

John Wright Sorry. Right sorry.
Thomas Percy Don't worry, what does she know?
Catesby She knows to keep her mouth shut which is more than some.
Thomas Percy But we only said ——
Catesby You say one more word and I'll nail you to the bottom barrel and sing hallelujah when you go up. Got that? Where's the other one, the quiet guy?
Thomas Wintour He stayed to keep an eye on the place.
Catesby Thank God somebody's showing a bit of sense.
Thomas Wintour We do have good news.
Catesby It better be.
Thomas Wintour I was furthest down the tunnel, and I heard a scraping noise on the other side of the foundation.
Thomas Percy This is so brilliant.
Thomas Wintour I got myself cleaned up and asked around.
Catesby So?
Thomas Wintour The cellar room right underneath the Lords Chamber was being cleared. The tenant was moving out.
Catesby Good God! Is it for hire?
Thomas Wintour No.
Catesby Damn.

Thomas Percy puts a piece of paper on the table

Thomas Percy Because I've already hired it. Mine for the year.

Catesby You lovely boy! You lovely lovely boy!
Thomas Wintour No more need to tunnel, and we can get the powder in a much better position.
Thomas Percy There's just one thing, I don't have the money to pay the rent.
Catesby No, of course you haven't. Fix him up some money, Thomas.
Thomas Wintour And that's the bad news. You're nearly broke.
Catesby Broke?
Thomas Wintour You're running this place, your Warwick place, your Lambeth place and John Whynniard's place, and you've bought all the equipment ——
John Wright — an' us board and lodge comes out of your pocket.
Thomas Wintour You can't do it alone. Knocking out the government isn't a one-man crusade.
Thomas Percy There's all sorts of people who'd put money up.
Thomas Wintour We're also going to need people to help us take over, otherwise who knows who might muscle in.
John Wright Our kid would join us like a shot.
Thomas Wintour Yes, and my brother too, and my brother-in-law.
Catesby All right. Sound them out, but be careful. Very careful.

They go leaving Catesby

More people. More mouths to go blabbing. Sweet Jesus, what have I started?

Catesby exits

The Lights fade to Black-out. The sign goes out

Music 8. A few bars from "The Quiet Guy" introduction play (*No scenery is necessary for the next scene*)

Scene 6

The Parlour

The Lights come up on King James and Robert Cecil who is reading some papers. He passes one to King James

Cecil My Lord, look at this report from the Midlands.
King James These Catholic gangs are getting worse!
Cecil I warned you, you're too soft on them. A lot of them openly carry swords now.

King James Swords?
Cecil Or daggers. Or knives or open blades or just generally pointy metal things ——
King James Stoppit stoppit stoppit.
Cecil Oh silly me. I forgot, you don't like naked steel do you?
King James I can't help it. My mother's friend Rizzio was stabbed to death right in front of her just before I was born. I was peculiarly affected you know. In fact, between you and me, I still am. I wear dagger-proof breeches. (*He indicates his breeches*) Feel that.

But Cecil's attention is elsewhere, he is comparing two particular pieces of paper with lists on them

Cecil Three dozen powder barrels? Three *dozen*?
King James Are you listening, Salisbury? What is that?
Cecil Store checks from the tower armoury.
King James Never mind your silly shopping lists. How can we stop these Catholics without a civil war?
Cecil Quite right, sire, that would not be the way. Destroying their bodies is not the answer, we need to destroy the cause.
King James How?
Cecil (*deliberately tearing the two lists to shreds*) I think there is a way that they might self-destruct.

The Lights fade

Music: 9. A few bars from "The Quiet Guy" introduction play to cover the change

Scene 7

The Cabaret Club

The Lights come up. The sign is on

Catesby and Thomas Wintour are seated at a table, around them are the other conspirators: Robert Wintour, John Grant, John Wright, Christopher Wright, Everard Digby, Thomas Percy, Ambrose Rookwood, Robert Keyes, Guy Fawkes. Thomas Bates watches the door

There is a "plan" on the wall — which is a simple drawing showing barrels of gunpowder under the House of Lords. Catesby rises to his feet

Catesby Thanks for making it, all of you. Just so's you know, I've already spoken individually to each person in this room, and you're all aware of why we're here. For those of you who haven't met before, this is your chance. Tom will give you the details.

Catesby sits, Thomas Wintour rises

Thomas Wintour Thank you, Sir Robin. By now you will all be familiar with this (*he indicates the plan*) and our target date is now confirmed as the Lords meeting on November the Fifth. The minute the bang goes off, we move in fast and take over. The main force will come from the Midlands and in charge is Sir Everard Digby.
Digby What-ho, chaps!
Thomas Wintour Your priority is to snatch the little Princess Elizabeth, but don't scare her.
Digby But I say, won't she be a tad rattled when she finds her father's had this explosion thingy?
Thomas Wintour Sing her a song, buy her a pony or something, but keep her sweet. We might need to put her on the throne.
Digby And make her into our bally own Queen what? Good egg.

Some of the others are getting irritated

John Wright Who invited "Everard"?
Catesby I did, and I invited Ambrose Rookwood here too.
John Grant "Ambrose"?
Catesby Before you get cheeky—on a horse he's the fastest thing in Europe.
Thomas Wintour What's more, he's making his superb stables available to us.
Rookwood Rather! The complete tally-ho pip pip. Everybody will just think it's one of my hunting binges.
Digby I say, wizard wheeze, Ambers.
Rookwood Bingo Diggers!
Thomas Wintour Quite. Next is John Grant, married to my sister——
Thomas Percy She must be prettier than you then.

There is a general small laugh

John Grant And she smells better than you.

There is a big laugh at Thomas Percy's expense

Thomas Wintour John's fixing the gear. Muskets, armour, powder...

John Grant Already sorted back at my place.
Digby But what if anyone comes looking?
Thomas Wintour He doesn't encourage visitors, do you, John?
John Grant Not a lot.
John Wright
Chris Wright } (*together*) Very wise.
Thomas Wintour On the front line we have the Wright brothers John and Chris, or Jack and Kit as they get called.
John Wright
Chris Wright } (*together*) How do.
Rookwood Spiffing. Which is which?
Chris Wright He's t'other one.
John Wright And I'm not.
Digby Sorry, I'm not sure I followed that.
Thomas Wintour Moving on, this is my brother Robert and he's working with Tom Percy here sounding out extra Catholic backup. Robert?

Thomas Wintour flicks something at Robert Wintour who is daydreaming

Robert Wintour Eh? Oh yeah, right. Hi, you guys. Me and Tom the backup situation, that's cool.
Thomas Wintour And this is Misery, or as his mother calls him, Robert Keyes.

Everybody sniggers at Robert Keyes

Chris Wright Misery?
John Wright What's up with him?
Chris Wright Oy, give us a smile, Sweetlips.

In a flash Robert Keyes gets up and has Chris Wright pinned by the throat

Thomas Wintour Just a word of warning. If you see Misery go for his sword, that might be the last thing you do see.

Robert Keyes releases Chris Wright then sits again

John Wright
Chris Wright } (*together*) I like him.

Everyone laughs except Keyes who looks as dour as ever

Thomas Wintour Over by the door, you'll know Sir Robin's man, Bates.

Bates Thanks to your gentlemenships, and how very I is gentlemennied to be in this gentlemanness what you is gentlemen doing.
Thomas Wintour Super. Right, that's the introductions done.

Thomas Wintour is about to sit

John Grant Not quite. Who's he?
Robert Wintour Who's who?
Thomas Wintour Oh yes, sorry Guy. This, everybody, is Guido Fawkes, ex-Catholic army and as you might have noticed, he comes with one especially interesting attribute.
Digby Gosh! What's that?
Thomas Wintour He's quiet.
All *Quiet*?
Thomas Wintour Not just quiet. He's very, very quiet.

Thomas Wintour sits and Catesby rises

Catesby Thank you, Thomas, but one last word. I'd like to thank you all for your contributions to the funds.
Digby But I could only drag up fifteen hundred pounds.
Catesby That was a lot, Everard. You done well.
John Grant Have we got enough?
Thomas Wintour I'm still waiting to hear from one or two others.
Bates Sir — it's Mr Tresham.
Catesby Let him in.

Francis Tresham enters with a mysterious girlfriend — Lily Gage

Tresham Sorry I'm late, everybody.
Catesby Good to see you, Francis.
Thomas Percy What's she doing here?
Tresham This is my companion ——
Thomas Percy Lily Gage! You mean to say you stood me up for Tresham?
John Wright Shut th'gob, Tom.
Tresham So. What's this little meeting all about?
Thomas Percy Not in front of her.
Thomas Wintour He's got a point, Sir Robin.
Thomas Percy Reliable she ain't. You know she was supposed to meet me the other night but ——
Chris Wright *Oy*! Our kid telt thee to shut it.
Catesby Sorry Francis, but this isn't for the lady.

Lily Gage turns and notices the plan. A whole lot of the conspirators jump up and stand in front of it to block her view. They try to whistle nonchalantly

Tresham Now I *am* interested. Sorry, my dear, but would you mind? Powder your nose or something.

Lily Gage looks round in wry amusement then goes

Thomas Percy I say he powders his nose too. Hands up who agrees.

All but Catesby and Thomas Wintour put their hands up

Thomas Wintour The man is pledging two thousand pounds.

A general gasp of amazement

Catesby He has a right to know where his money is going.
Thomas Wintour So who's still got his hand up now?

All except Thomas Percy and Robert Keyes put their hands down and sit. The Wright brothers pull Thomas Percy down

What is it, Misery?
Robert Keyes Just a thought. There's already twelve men in this room who know about this.
Thomas Wintour So?
Robert Keyes He'll be the thirteenth man.
Digby Sorry old chap, not quite with you.
Rookwood Completely adrift.
Robert Keyes There were thirteen men at the Last Supper when our Lord was betrayed. Thirteen is a bad number.
Thomas Wintour Oh come on, Mr Keyes, the Treshams are a good Catholic family.
Thomas Percy Who says?
Catesby *I do*! He is my cousin, all right? Besides, Francis has seen us together in this room. Therefore he's in.
Robert Keyes Or he's dead.
Tresham Dead?
All Dead.

10: The Quiet Guy

For this song the conspirators are split into two groups, Thomas Wintour, John Wright, Chris Wright, Thomas Percy and Catesby are Group A. The rest are Group B. Until the first chorus they are all addressing Tresham

Catesby Dangerous deeds have already been done
All We can't go back now
Catesby Words have occurred that could see us all hung
All We can't retract now
Group A Piece by little piece
Group B And bit by little bit
All Slowly the elements start to fit all together
Catesby But now we need a volunteer
To execute the plan
Whose mind is clear, who knows no fear
A most amazing man.

Group A	**Group B**
Who won't panic if	Who …
The guards come along?	The guards come along?
Who won't run off if	Who …
He thinks it's going wrong?	He thinks it's going wrong?

All Who's the best at staying still and silent?
Who's the one they're never going to find?
Who can we depend to the very end?
Who's the one on whom we can rely?
The Quiet Guy. That's who.

Thomas Percy Why should it be him who gets the credit
All he has to do is sit
And see the fuse is safely lit.
Catesby Brother would you like to take his place?
All Well would you?
Catesby The powder
All (*shouting*) *Bang*!
Catesby Might go up in your face.
All It could do
Catesby Supposing you were caught,
You know what they would do
So give it careful thought before you say this job's for you

Catesby (*speaking*) Well?

Thomas Percy shakes his head

Group A	**Group B**
Who has what it takes	Who …
To wait in the dark?	To wait in the dark?
Whose hand won't shake as	Who …
He strikes up the spark?	He strikes up the spark?

All
Who would never talk if he was taken?
Who would never give us all away?
Who would never crack even on the rack?
Who's the one on whom we can rely?
The Quiet Guy. That's …

Group A	**Group B**
Who won't panic if	Who …
The guards come along?	The guards come along?
Who won't run off if	Who …
He thinks it's going wrong?	He thinks it's going wrong?

All
Who's the best at staying still and silent?
Who's the one they're never going to find?
Who can we depend
To the very end?
Who's the one on whom we can rely?
The Quiet Guy
That's Who!

Tresham approaches Catesby to chat, meanwhile the other conspirators all go to congratulate Guy, they take down the plan and straighten the room out

Guy Fawkes is helped off by all except Rookwood and Thomas Wintour who happen to hang back and hear the end of the exchange

Tresham (*speaking*) Sorry Robin, but I don't like it.
Catesby Hah! Too late. You're in it.
Tresham But my sister's husband sits in the Lords. Your cousin by marriage.
Catesby My cousin?
Tresham Mounteagle. I can't be paying to blow him up.
Catesby That name Mounteagle again!
Tresham At least we could warn him to keep away.

Rookwood I say, if you're warning people, I've got a few jolly decent chums in there, all Catholics too.
Catesby I see. Does anybody else have friends sucking up to King Wimp?
Thomas Wintour Well actually…
Catesby Oh not you, Tom! Soon we'll be putting up posters saying "*Keep out*, Live Gunpowder in cellar." How about that?

Dorothy looks in

Dorothy Sir Robin, Catherine asks if you've finished?
Catesby Yes thank you, Dot. Off you go, boys, and remember, absolute silence. If Mounteagle goes up too, then tough.

All go leaving Dorothy, who is horror-struck at what she's just heard

Catherine and the chorus come on and find she's started singing

11: Nothing!

Dorothy	I don't want to believe what I hear Is it destruction for the man I hold dear?
Catherine	Maybe, but maybe you've Picked up the message all wrong.
Dorothy	But the voices were worried and hushed And their actions were nervous and rushed If there's the tiniest chance that I'm right all along, all along…
Catherine	You never heard even a single word
Chorus	You know nothing
Catherine	You didn't catch even the faintest snatch
Chorus	You know nothing
Catherine	So walk away, spend your day Doing all the little things that you'd be doing anyway.
Dorothy	I can't live when I fear for that man I've got to give him every chance that I can I've got this feeling a tragedy's going to start
Catherine	Take a warning, you don't want to know What you overheard, you must let it go
Dorothy	I haven't a choice, 'cos I know that I must play my part, play my part

Chorus You never caught even a single thought
You know nothing
You never saw what went behind the door
You know nothing.
If you mess with fate don't underestimate
How little love is worth beside a barrel full of hate.

You never heard even a single word
You know nothing
You didn't catch even the faintest snatch
You know nothing.

So lay it low and let it go,
There's only one thing that you know
And that one thing you know is you know
Nothing.

Dorothy runs off

Black-out

The others go

Scene 8

Lord Mounteagle's House, Hoxton

The Lights come up. The sign is off, no scenery is necessary

Mounteagle comes on with his napkin in his collar

Mounteagle Bagwich? Have you got that wine? Bagwich?

Bagwich the servant ambles on holding a piece of paper

Bagwich No.
Mounteagle But you went hours ago.
Bagwich All right, I'll go again. Never mind the urgent message.
Mounteagle Message? What message?
Bagwich The *urgent* one from the tall bloke.
Mounteagle What tall bloke?
Bagwich The tall bloke that gave me the message. Oh, what's the point. I'll get the wine. I'm only the servant.

Mounteagle What's the message?
Bagwich Oh, so you want it now? Right, well it's — er — oh, you've got me all confused now — hang on, I'll think of it.

Mounteagle sees the piece of paper Bagwich is holding

Mounteagle Is that it?
Bagwich Oh. Yeah. That's it.

Mounteagle takes the paper

Mounteagle It isn't signed.
Bagwich Don't blame me. I was getting wine not messages.
Mounteagle I can hardly make it out.
Bagwich That's your problem. I've got to get the wine. (*To the audience*) This wine doesn't actually affect the plot much, so you won't be seeing me again. Mind, why should you care? I'm only the servant.

Bagwich shuffles off

Mounteagle reads the letter

Mounteagle "My Lord. Out of the love I bear to some of your friends ——

As Mounteagle continues to read the Lights fade to allow a scene change to the Palace. We hear his voice read the message during the change

— I have a care of your preservation. Therefore I would advise you, as you tender your life, to devise some excuse to shift of your attendance at this Parliament, for God and man hath concurred to punish the wickedness of this time. And think not slightly of this advertisement but retire yourself into your country, where you may expect the event in safety ——

Scene 9

In the Palace

By the time the lights come up Mounteagle is reading to Robert Cecil

— For though there be no appearance of any sir, yet I say they shall receive a terrible blow this Parliament, and yet they shall not see who hurts them. This council is not to be condemned because it may do you good and can do you no harm, for the danger is passed as soon as you have burned the letter."

Cecil But you didn't burn it, did you?
Mounteagle Not yet, Sir Robert.
Cecil Not ever, Mounteagle. This message ties in with certain information I have received.
Mounteagle But what does it mean?
Cecil The King has a fortunate judgement in solving riddles, I think he will enjoy this one.

King James enters with the sniggering Groom

King James What will I enjoy — you stooped little Drummock?
Groom Oooh, hark at himself!
King James Did you like that?
Groom Like it? It's enough to twist my britches.
Cecil "This Parliament shall receive a terrible blow, and yet they shall not see who hurts them."
King James What?
Cecil An anonymous note came.
King James Do we take it seriously?
Cecil We do, My Lord.
King James Oh why do they all seek to finish me? Am I not loved?
Cecil Overwhelmingly.
Groom Especially by stooped little Drummocks.
King James A terrible blow, and shall not see who hurts them? It's powder.
Mounteagle Sire?
King James Gunpowder! The coward's weapon, the same that killed the Earl of Darnley.
Cecil Do you wish me to investigate?
King James Oh yes yes, my good friend Robert, Earl of Salisbury. How I appreciate all you do for me.
Cecil First we must find where they've put it.
Mounteagle Oh I say, let me look. After all, it was me that got the note.
Cecil Very well, but get on with it. I've been looking forward to this.

Mounteagle and Cecil go off

King James is about to follow, but the Groom interrupts him

Groom So who's the Earl of Darnley when he's at home?
King James He was my father. Well, he probably was.

King James exits

Groom Probably he says.

The Groom grins cheekily at the audience then exits

The Lights fade to Black-out

You may wish to play the extended intro music for "Thirty-Six Barrels" (12a) to cover the scene change and then go directly into the song

SCENE 10

The Lights come up on The Cellars

Robert Wintour starts singing. During the first lines all the other conspirators except Catesby come on and listen. (Fawkes, Thomas Wintour, John Grant, John Wright, Christopher Wright, Everard Digby, Thomas Percy, Ambrose Rookwood, Robert Keyes, Bates)

12b: Thirty-Six Barrels

Robert Wintour There's a new horizon dawning
Lighting up a revolution
Soon we'll see a brighter morning
A better day with a new solution.

Finally Catesby comes on and isn't impressed to see them all sitting round singing

All (*except Catesby*) All too long, we've waited in the dark
Now we've got a light to guide us
Down the path so long denied us
Are you ready?
Are you ready?

Catesby Then *go*!

The conspirators start bringing on gunpowder barrels and singing loudly

All See what we've got
The powder plot it's the powder powder plot
Life's getting hot
For the powder plot for the powder powder plot.

Catesby Quiet! Keep it quiet
When you creep across the yard
Thomas Wint. Quiet, be very quiet
So we don't disturb the guard
All Quiet, be deadly quiet
Because we don't want a single soul to know we're here.

The Chorus all come on in the background at this point and start singing

Chorus Yes we're here! Yes we're here,
We're here, we're here!

During the refrain, the conspirators creep about assembling their barrels while the chorus sing. Bates keeps a lookout

We've got thirty-six barrels of fun
Thirty-six reasons to run
We're rocking, shocking, knocking them down
Tonight we're going to light up the town

We've got thirty-six barrels of fun
To raise the roof to the sun
Make a date to come out and play
We're gon-na blow your blues aw…
Bates *Watch out*! We're not alone, I said
Watch out! Our cover's blown.

The conspirators hurriedly pile the barrels up and throw old sacks over them, which have sticks attached, to make the whole thing look like a pile of firewood

Catesby Quick, stick the gear
Slip out of here
Let the quiet guy
Stay and keep an eye.

Mounteagle and his assistant saunter on

All conspirators line up and force smiles. Fawkes is left by the pile

Conspirators Face the front
Look nonchalant
Act casual
Just as you will.

The conspirators try and shuffle off past Mounteagle, each one speaking to him as he goes past

Bates 'Evening guv.
John Grant Heavens above.
Robert Wintour It's getting late.
Chris Wright We just can't wait.
Rookwood Bye bye old fruit.
Digby Pip pip toot toot.

The conspirators are just about off when they see Mounteagle go up to Fawkes, and poke at the disguised pile

Mounteagle You, fellow there, what are you up to?

The conspirators rush back in panic

Thomas Percy Johnson — his name is Johnson
And he is just a passer by
Thomas Wint. Johnson — Johnny Johnson
He's just an ordinary guy
All Johnson — Mr Johnson
John Grant He's a harmless bloke, there's nothing going on.

Mounteagle turns to go

Catesby So you can go.
John Wright On your way.
Chris Wright Bog off.

Mounteagle and his assistant exit

Bates They've gone …

Everybody springs to life again, they start setting up the barrels properly

Chorus And we've got thirty-six barrels of fun
Thirty-six reasons to run
We're rocking, shocking, knocking them down
Tonight we're going to light up the town.

During the next verse, Mounteagle and Cecil appear briefly in deep conversation, Cecil showing great interest in what he is being told, before they both go

We've got thirty-six barrels of fun
To raise the roof to the sun
Make a date to come out and play
We're gon-na blow your blues aw…

Although Mounteagle and Cecil have gone Catesby is nervy!

Catesby Quiet! I said be quiet
Digby Do you think they're coming back?
Catesby Quiet — and I mean quiet!
Robert Keyes Do you want to face the rack?
Catesby Quiet — quiet quiet
John Grant It's in your mind, there's no-one else about
Digby So we can talk
Rookwood And we can sing …
All And dance and shout that …

In this last refrain the barrels are finally fixed up, fuses attached and Fawkes is left beside them

Chorus We've got thirty-six barrels of fun
Thirty-six reasons to run
We're rocking, shocking, knocking them down
Tonight we're going to light up the town

We've got thirty-six barrels of fun
To raise the roof to the sun
Make a date to come out and play
We're gon-na blow your blues away!

They all go off

Cecil and Mounteagle and some heavies come on and seize Fawkes

Cecil This is where the party really starts.

Music: 13. Reprise a few last chords of the song to finish

CURTAIN

ACT II

Scene 1

The Tower

14: One Hell of a Guy

The sign is off. Dark music starts. Dim lighting comes up on Fawkes who is slumped in a chair, tied up. Two shadowy figures (Matthew and Eunice) loom over him

Sir Robert Cecil enters

Cecil Prisoner, you still refuse to speak?
Prisoner, the human body's weak

Prisoner, you know we can break you in the end
So what is there to gain
From so much pain?

Prisoner, I think it's time you knew
What we're prepared to do to you.

The music pauses for a couple of bars

Eunice Grrr!

The music resumes

Matthew Hey, did you hear her? Do it again, Eunice.
Eunice *Grrr*!
Cecil Well?
Matthew It's no good, boss. We've had him two days and we just ain't getting through.

The Chorus enters, the mood completely lifts

The Lighting brightens

Chorus Nothing is troubling him, he sleeps pretty well
There isn't a cloud in his sky
He's calm, he's collected, he don't make a fuss
How does he do it?

Eunice
Matthew } (*together*) It's a mystery to us

Chorus He's down on his luck, but a loser he ain't
He's smiling the world in the eye
It seems an awful shame
We don't even know his name
He's just one hell of a guy.

Cecil You know you're trying my patience?
Chorus Temper temper
Cecil I'm going to count up to three

Chorus (*shouted*) One two three

Cecil Now you've done it,
You've really gone and done it.

Matthew
Eunice } (*together*) You're going to see

Chorus Him stamp his feet and throw a wobbly
Cecil Admit you're guilty of treason
Chorus Treason.
Cecil This is your very last chance
Chorus Wooo!
Cecil Why won't you listen to reason?
Chorus Call him mad, call him rude

Matthew
Eunice } (*together*) He's just not in a chatty mood 'cos

Chorus Nothing is troubling him, he sleeps pretty well
There isn't a cloud in his sky
He's calm, he's collected, he don't make a fuss
How does he do it?
It's a mystery to us.

He's down on his luck, but a loser he ain't
He's smiling the world in the eye
It seems an awful shame
We don't even know his name

And he's not going to tell
He's holding out well
'Cos he's just one hell of a guy.

Black-out

They all go off

SCENE 2

The Cabaret Club

The Lights come up. The sign is on. Catesby and Thomas Wintour are interrogating Tresham, who is being held by John Wright and Chris Wright

Catesby Let's go over it again. Somebody sent a note.
Tresham Not me.
Thomas Wintour A note to Mounteagle. Your brother-in-law.
Tresham It could have been anyone.
Catesby And right now Fawkes is in the tower. God knows how much longer he can hold out.
John Wright And how long canst thee hold out?
Tresham Me?
Chris Wright We'll crack thee in five minutes.
John Wright What's tha' say, Sir Robin?
Tresham No!
Chris Wright Just five nasty little minutes.
Tresham Sir Robert — why would I write such a note? I'm in it as deep as the rest of you.
Catesby Are you?
Thomas Wintour So far you haven't even tried to leave London, and yet no-one's hassling you.
Tresham Or you for that matter.
Thomas Wintour Oh no? They've pulled in my servants, and there's already a warrant out for Thomas Percy. Ambrose is riding north to warn everyone.
Catesby And yet you stay quietly in London, watching the fun out of your window.
John Wright Becost thee sent the note.
Tresham No no no!

Tresham bangs the trick table for emphasis

Henry Garnet comes out from underneath the table. He has a frying pan and is wearing an apron

Garnet Blinkin' Nora, what's the commotion?
Catesby Henry! Just the man we need. Do you think he sent the note?
Chris Wright Well?
Garnet No.
Chris Wright How dost tha' know?
Garnet He wouldn't send a warning ten days early, would he? He'd do it at the last minute so word couldn't get further.
Tom Wintour Why would he care about that?
Garnet Because his money's in this. If he sent the whole thing down, he'd go down with it.
Tom Wintour That follows.
Garnet Besides, he wouldn't send a note anyway. Notes have a habit of reaching the wrong people. No, if anything he'd give the man a whisper in his ear. For my money, the geezer's straight.

Wright reluctantly releases Tresham

Catesby Thanks, Henry.

Garnet looks at his pan

Garnet It's all gone cold now.

Garnet goes back under the trick table

Thomas Wintour Someone's here.

Lily Gage enters

Tresham Ah Lily, perfect timing. If there's nothing else, gentlemen?
John Wright Still with him?
Chris Wright What dost tha' see in him?
Lily Everything I look for.

Tresham and Lily exit

Thomas Wintour So what happens now, Robin?
Catesby We've come too far to go back. Everard Digby's got the Midlands all set to rise up, so let's do it.
Thomas Wintour But Digby won't make his move until he knows the King is dead.

Catesby Then that's what I'll tell him — and you make sure you back me up. Either we win or we swing, there's no choice.

Catherine Wheel, Jennie and Maggie enter

Catherine Wheel Robin! They'll find you here!
Catesby Shhh! We're gone already.
Thomas Wintour You haven't seen us.
Chris Wright I'm invisible.
John Wright Who said that?

Catesby, Thomas Wintour and the Wrights go off

Catherine Wheel Poor Robin, he's still upset about that note.
Maggie The note? What note?
Jenny Haven't you heard? Somebody sent a note to Lord Mounteagle. Didn't want him sitting on thirty-six barrels.
Maggie Who'd be daft enough to send a note?
Jenny Oh come on, it's obvious. Who do we know who's nuts about the bloke?
Catherine Wheel Watch it, girls. Gossip doesn't help anyone.
Jenny Oh, I'm not saying it definitely was Dorothy, in fact only last night some bloke was asking me about it.
Catherine Wheel Bloke? What bloke?
Jenny Just some punter, up from Kent, said he knew her, in fact he took her off.
Catherine Wheel Took her off?
Jenny She was making like she didn't want to go with him, but you know how prissy she is.
Maggie Jen! What did you say?
Jenny Said? I was just chatting.
Maggie You know her family's from Kent, they're all heavy Catholics too. And friends of Sir Robin.
Jenny You don't think he believed me do you?

Black-out. The sign goes off

The girls exit

Music 15. An instrumental piece of "Nothing!" plays to cover the scene change

Scene 3

Ingham Mote

There is a small archway, which is the entrance to a space a bit like a walk-in cupboard. Some shadowy figures including Mary, Jack, Jane and Alice drag Dorothy on, her hands are bound, she has been locked up without food or water for a long time

Dorothy Speak to me — speak one of you! Please, a cup of water! Why are you doing this to me?

As Dorothy pleads she is shoved into the "cupboard" opening

Why don't you speak? Mary, why don't you speak?

One figure hesitates

Of course I know it's you. And that's Jack, and you, Jane my own sister! What are you doing?

A figure speaks to the others

Mary Hold her. Come on, Jack.
Dorothy Mary, Jack — why?

Mary and Jack go

Dorothy Jane, talk to me! You are killing me.

One of the remaining figures stiffens

Jane, dear Jane, please, what have I done?
Jane We are forbidden to talk to you.
Dorothy But why?
Jane The letter to Mounteagle.
Alice They're coming.

Mary and Jack return with some buckets of cement or other building stuff

Mary You were not to speak!

Mary slaps Jane

Jane She has a right to know.
Jack She knows already.
Dorothy What do I know?
Jack You betrayed the plot and all English Catholics.
Dorothy I betrayed no-one.
Mary Your note, your silly girlish love-struck note — thanks to you the King and his Parliament live on.
Dorothy In this world is it such a sin to save a life?

Mary and Jack start walling up the opening with Dorothy behind it

What are you doing?
Mary You have brought eternal shame on our family. We have no choice but to deny your very existence. From now on, you were never born, you never lived and you never died.

Jane and Alice are sobbing

Do you want to join her? Then get to it.

Jane and Alice help brick up the wall

You brick me in? How will I see? Eat? Breathe …

16: The Girl That Never Was

For the song, the "family" comprises of Mary, Jane, Alice, Jack. The chorus of the song should be enhanced by voices off stage, or by bringing the chorus on to sing in the background

Family Two tons of stone and mortar
We'll soon forget the daughter
Who brought the shame
To the family name.

Take her picture from the wall
Take her clothes, destroy them all
If we're asked we don't know her at all.

Chorus There'll be no-one to mourn for a girl never born
There'll be no marble stone saying here lies her bones
She'll be out of our lives altogether because
She's the girl that never was.

Dorothy My eyes are closed, yet I can see
An angel reaching down for me
My weight is gone, I feel my body fly.

Above the wind, and above the rain
Floating where there is no pain
Just the light about me as I'm walking on the sky

Chorus Lay the table one less place
Spread the rest to fill the space
Shut out every clue to our disgrace

Wipe your mind of her looks
Rip her name out of books
And erase every trace of her form and her face
She'll be out of our lives altogether because
She's the girl that never was.

Dorothy Looking down so far below
The world is shrinking as I go
Nothing left to hurt me here on high.

I close my hands, and I say a prayer
I can feel you standing there
Hand in hand together we'll be walking on the sky.

Add extra voices

Ahh, Ahh, Ahh, Ahh, Ahh, Ahh.

The last brick goes in. Dorothy is walled up

The Lights fade to Black-out

All exit

The music continues to the finish, for the scene change

SCENE 4

The King's Boudoir

As the Lights fade up we find King James is having his hair combed by the Groom. James is brooding

Groom Well, for myself I do like a big ruff, but please me, you don't want to get caught in the rain or next thing you know, it's flopping round your neck like a dead seagull. There's only one thing worse in my book and that's having too many slashes in your britches. I tell you, you show me Walter Raleigh and I'll show you a man whose undies have seen the world, and vice versa if you get my meaning ——

King James I could have been blown into a million pieces.

Groom What? Oh yeah, that. Occupational hazard innit? — What with you being King and all. Mind, don't tell me about occupational hazards. I caught my nail the other day. Look.

King James A million pieces!

Groom Oh my dear!

King James Right now the crows would be pecking me off Westminster roof.

King James briefly thinks he is getting some sympathy, but the Groom is actually focused on his hair

Groom Split ends! Don't they just make you want to die? Never mind, I'll rub in some goose droppings, we'll soon have you bouffant again. Honestly, I can't think of anything worse, well apart from dandruff of course ——

Queen Anne enters

Anne My Lord?

Groom The Queen! Please madam, can't you see himself is going to bed?

King James Annie! How are you, my dear?

Groom Don't come any closer. She'll be wanting to get pregnant again, sire.

King James Oh dear. Are you terribly desperate?

Anne Not just yet.

Groom Fibber.

King James Leave us alone.

Groom Oh I couldn't! Not just the two of you, not in the bedroom!

King James She is my wife.

Groom She's still a woman.

The Groom exits

King James and Anne turn out to be extremely fond of each other

Anne I had to come and see you, James. I was so worried for you.

King James Me? Why?

Anne This awful plot. It was so close.
King James Yes Annie, it was close. You nearly had your chance this time.
Anne Chance? What chance?
King James You could have married again. You could have found a man more fitting to take a wife than myself.
Anne Let's not have that conversation again. You know how I feel.

She sings unaccompanied, loosely fitting the words to the tune of "He's a Man"

Anne
You don't go fighting wars so you're my man.
You don't treat me like a whore so you're my man.
Your children all adore you
And I'll always be here for you
You're my man, you're my very special man.

King James You silly Queen!
Anne Look who's talking. I don't want to lose you.
King James Remember that conspiracy of northern witches who made wax dummies of me?
Anne They even sacrificed some cats, didn't they?

They laugh

King James See Annie, most of my enemies are pathetic.
Anne But some are not. What about that man in the Tower?
King James The quiet one, he's a real mystery. He's got some very curious scars on his body and apparently he speaks French although who can tell?
Anne In Europe they can always force a prisoner to talk.
King James I've a man who could force him, if I give my permission.
Anne Then do it!
King James But the conspiracy is already broken.
Anne James, you need arrests. You need confessions. You need to be rid of the Catholics or they will try again and again and again.
King James But Annie, you're a Catholic!
Anne So? Look at me, James, I am your wife Annie. I don't want to be a widow and I don't want my children to lose their father.

King James sits and starts to scribble a letter as he shouts

King James *You can come back in now*! Come on, I know you're listening at the door.

The Groom sticks his head round

I want you to take a message to the Tower.
Groom The Tower? Who's it for?
King James The Lieutenant.
Groom No!
King James Yes. Take this to Sir William Waad.

We hear some screams as the Lights fade to Black-out

They all exit

Music 17. Some intro music from "One Hell of a Guy" plays to cover the scene change

SCENE 5

The Cabaret Club

The sign is on. During the Black-out the illusion equipment has been set up (see "staging suggestions" p.79). To start with this equipment is covered with a cloth

The Lights come up dimly to reveal Matthew and Eunice guarding the equipment

Catherine Wheel enters and steps into a small spotlight which comes on

Catherine Wheel Ladies and gentlemen, there are many different aspects to entertainment including comedy, music, drama, mime, and occasionally just a touch of the bizarre. What we are about to present may not be to everybody's taste, but I'm sure you'll agree that what you will see in the next few minutes you will remember for the rest of your lives.
Matthew Whatever happens, stay in your seats.
Eunice Or we take you round the office.
Catherine Wheel Ladies and gentlemen, direct from the Tower of London, Sir William Waad.

The very spooky Sir William Waad enters, he is holding a nasty-looking implement

Waad Good-evening, and may I say what a pleasure it is to be here by Royal Appointment. You may be wondering if I shall require volunteers for audience participation. However, you may relax, I already have a volunteer.

Before we commence though, I am sure you will wish to hear a letter I received from the King.

He opens a letter

"The gentler tortures are to be first used, *et sic per gradus ad ima tenditur*" — which of course means "and so on to the very worst". The King is gracious enough to conclude by saying "and so God speed your good work". Behold.

Music 18. There is a brief drum roll as Waad pulls the cloth away. As the equipment is revealed we hear some chords and some of the intro music from "One Hell of a Guy" is played. We see the dummy spread-eagled with arms and legs tied by four ropes. (See "staging suggestions" p.79). If necessary some shadowy figures enter and help to work the illusion by pulling the ropes

Begin.

The ropes are very gradually pulled. The dummy stretches and stretches! Waad is paying close attention, then suddenly he waves his hand to stop the music

Wait!

He listens intently, putting his ear to the dummy's mouth. He then announces

Kindly inform Sir Robert Cecil that Fawkes Talks.

19: Fawkes Talks

The Chorus run on and sing (if necessary striking the illusion scene at the same time). Some lines are shouted out as solos

All Fawkes talks!
Solo Whatever did they do to him?
All Fawkes talks!
Solo Did he give us all away?
All Fawkes talks!
Solo What are we supposed to do?
All Fawkes talks!
We'll have to
Sit tight and keep down and anxiously pray
The stench of suspicion does not blow this way.

If only we could be grabbing our bags
And getting out of this mess
Hitch a ride on a promising tide
To a confidential address.

We didn't ask to get into this
But we're in up to our necks
Now that

Fawkes talks!
Fawkes talks!
Fawkes talks!
Fawkes talks!

We want to
Pack up and clear out but it can't be done
There's no-one to hide us and nowhere to run.

If only we could be hitting the road to
Start up again elsewhere
Business has to continue as normal
Like we haven't a care.

We didn't ask to get into this
But we're in up to our necks
Now that

Fawkes talks!

At the end of the song Catherine Wheel is left with Jenny and Maggie sitting to one side of the stage in a small pool of light. (*They should not be sitting at the trick table*)

Maggie Do you think Sir Robin will come back?
Catherine Wheel I doubt we'll see any of them again.
Jenny I wish we knew what had happened.
Maggie Look! Isn't that the miserable one?

A ragged looking Robert Keyes enters

Jenny Mr Keyes! What are you doing here?
Robert Keyes Someone had to come and tell you. It's all over.

The Waitress comes over

Waitress Good-evening and welcome to Catesby's. My name is ——
Catherine Wheel Not now, Denise. Just bring him a special.
Waitress Is that with ice or without ice, sir?
Catherine Wheel Go on!

The Waitress exits. At a suitable time she returns with a drink and goes again

Maggie Where are the others?
Robert Keyes I last saw them all heading north. Who were they kidding? — still trying to play at little heroes while their wives and families were being rounded up. I'd had enough, I went to check on the missus and I've been hiding out since. There's only me and Robert Wintour still out, and I don't fancy his chances any more than mine.
Catherine Wheel So what happened?
Robert Keyes According to Robert, first of all they met up with Everard Digby at Dunchurch, who'd got quite a force organized.

Music 20. Music starts for "A Thousand Angry Men"

The Lights come up on the main area for the following action with the conspirators which the girls and Robert Keyes watch. (*See "staging suggestions" p.79*)

Catesby enters with Thomas Wintour, Robert Wintour, Bates, Rookwood, John Wright, Chris Wright, John Grant and Thomas Percy. They meet up with Digby (*who has some extra soldiers with him if possible*)

Catesby Everard!
Digby Sir Robin! We're all ready oh by gosh yes indeedy-doo.

They all cheer

All (*singing*)
There's a thousand angry men a-riding by
There's a thousand hungry spirits flying high
There's no going back
Stand by to attack
There's a thousand angry men a-riding by.

The music continues

Digby Just a moment old chap.
Catesby What?

The music stops

Digby We rather thought there was to be some sort of explosion thingy in London first.
Catesby Have a bit of faith, Everard. That's where we've been clever.
Digby You mean, we're not having an explosion thingy now?
Men No explosion thingy?

Some of the extra men mutter things like "Oh well, forget it then." and drift off (and don't come back)

Catesby No! Come back! Look Everard, think about it, a big explosion would have been rather obvious, wouldn't it?
Digby By crikey, you're right.
Catesby Now they think they've stopped the explosion, they won't be expecting us to come charging in.
Digby Brilliant! But the King is dead, isn't he?
Catesby Oh yes, isn't he, Tom?
Thomas Wintour Er, yes. And Cecil too.
Digby Spiffing.
Catesby Come on then, let's see what we can get out of Warwick.

Music 21. Music starts for second verse "A Hundred Angry Men"

All *(singing)* There's a hundred angry men a-riding by
There's a hundred hungry spirits flying high
There's no going back
Stand by to attack
There's a hundred angry men a-riding by.

Robert Wintour Hey, stop, this isn't right. I make it sort of more like fifty.

The music comes to a stop again

Catesby And your point is…?
Robert Wintour We shouldn't have done that Warwick raid. It was a bad scene. All we scored was a few horses and a whole load of hassle, man.
Catesby Have a bit of faith, Robert! Bates, it's time to activate plan B.

Catesby passes Bates a note

Find Father Henry and get him to raise some muscle from Wales.
Bates What, Welsh Wales?

Catesby Absolutely.

Bates goes and knocks on the trick table

Henry Garnet comes out

Bates A letter for you, your Jesuitting Fatherness.

Garnet reads the note

Garnet Not Welsh Wales?
Bates Indeed, your Jesuitting Fatherness.
Garnet No way. If he's relying on help from Wales he's had it. I'm gone.

Garnet quickly chucks on another disguise, (suggest glasses with false nose?) grabs a case and hangs a sign saying "To Let" from the edge of the table

Garnet exits

John Grant So far so bad.
Rookwood Sir Robin, there's a large group trying to catch us up.
Catesby Aha! How many?
Rookwood Quite a lot.
Catesby There you are men! How about that?

Music 22

All (*singing*) Quite a lot of angry men are riding by
Quite a lot of hungry spirits flying high
There's no going back
Stand by to attack
Quite a lot of angry men are riding by.

We ride forward to freedom
We ride to forward our cause
So ride right up beside us
For the future to be yours
For the future to be yours.

Thomas Wintour So who's in charge of this group behind us?
Rookwood Sir Richard Walsh.

The music stops

John Grant Oh great. He's the High Sheriff of Worcestershire.
Digby Is that bad?
John Grant Bad? He's not coming to join us, he's coming to get us.
Catesby We best be ready for him then. We'll stop at Holbeach and rest up.

The Lights on the main area change to suggest indoor night-time

Robert Wintour Holbeach? Oh no that's really heavy. I had a kind of bad dream about that place.
Catesby Don't be silly, Robert! They won't reach us at Holbeach.
Robert Wintour No, this bad thing wasn't the enemy. But I know it was bad.

The men ignore Robert Wintour and flump to the ground and settle themselves down. Robert Wintour reluctantly joins them

Robert Keyes They should have listened to him. It turns out that the powder they'd been carrying was soaked, so they put it out in front of the fire to dry it ——
Catherine Wheel Gunpowder?
Maggie They tried to dry it in front of a fire?
Robert Keyes Don't forget they'd been riding for three days and nights. They couldn't think straight.
Catherine Wheel Well?

There is a small flash or bang

The conspirators scream. As the action continues, John Grant is having his eyes bandaged. The Lights on the main area rise as if outdoor daytime again

Robert Keyes Sir Robin got his explosion at last. None dead, but John Grant lost his eyesight. That's when it all really fell apart.

Music 23. An extended low-key intro to verse four starts

Catesby So, how many angry men are left?
Digby Sorry, Sir Robin. Got to take my chance. Family and everything you know.

Catesby waves Digby off

Robert Wintour Yeah, guess it's time to split, Sir Rob.
Thomas Wintour Sorry you got involved, Robert.

Robert Wintour Hey! So the party's over, but at least I got invited! You riding my way?
Thomas Wintour My place is with Robin.
Robert Wintour Right. Well it's been a gas, man. See you sometime, eh?
Thomas Wintour Do you think so?
Robert Wintour Course I do. You're my brother. That's how it works!

Digby and Robert Wintour leave the group

Bates also wants to go

Bates Please, Sir Robin …
Catesby Of course, Bates. My fault for dragging you in.

Bates goes

Catesby Go on, all of you.
John Wright Go! What for?
Chris Wright We like to see a thing through.
John Wright And so does Mr Percy here, don't tha' Tom?
Tom Percy Oh — er, yes, of course.
Chris Wright Besides, we've got to take care of our old pal Granty here.
John Grant And who asked you to? I'm only staying to look after you two great Yorkie puddings.
Catesby How about you, Ambrose?
Rookwood I'd rather have these three on my side than against me.
John Wright Tha's solid, Ambrose.
Chris Wright Ay, tha'll do for me.
Catesby We'll show them, eh lads?

Left huddled together are Catesby, John Wright, Chris Wright, Thomas Percy, John Grant, Ambrose Rookwood, Thomas Wintour. They start singing

All (*singing*)
There's several angry men a-riding by
There's several hungry spirits flying high
There's no going back
Stand by to attack
There's several angry men a-riding by.

Sir Richard Walsh enters. He can either have a few musketeers with him, or he can come on alone and we imagine them off to one side of the stage. The music halts as he shouts

Sir Richard Walsh Fire!

Sir Richard Walsh then immediately scurries away to a corner and sticks his fingers in his ears

Tom Wintour leaves the group to look out

Tom Wintour Did someone say fire?

Tom Wintour is shot in the arm and staggers back to the group. John and Chris Wright pull swords and advance

Chris Wright Like that is it?
John Wright Come down here.
Chris Wright If tha' reckons tha's hard enough.
John Wright I'll have thee, thee and then thee.
Chris Wright I'll tek three an' all for starters, so let's si' thee.

Unfortunately their swordsmanship is wasted. First John then Chris are shot and lie dead. Ambrose Rookwood wanders forward

Rookwood Now look here, you chaps, you could bally well see that they only had swords. There's certain things a chap simply does not do …

Rookwood gets shot and falls wounded. Left in the group are Catesby, Tom Wintour, Tom Percy and John Grant

Catesby Come on, boys. We'll stand together and die together.

(*Singing*) There's four very angry men a-riding by
Four very angry spirits riding high…

(*Speaking*) Sing up, you men!

One shot kills both Catesby and Thomas Percy

John Grant What was that?
Thomas Wintour They were killed with one shot!
John Grant One shot?
Catherine Wheel Is that right?
Robert Keyes Yes.
Catherine Wheel Good grief I have to see that again. Wind it back.

The action reverses at high speed. The Lights on the main area flicker

John Grant Shot one.
Thomas Wintour Shot one with killed were they.
John Grant That was what.

Catesby and Thomas Percy "get up backwards"

Catesby Men you up sing.
Catherine Wheel There. Now run it slowly.

The forwards action occurs again but very slowly with the words dragged out in low voices

Catesby Sing up, you men!

One shot kills Catesby and Thomas Percy

John Grant What was that?
Thomas Wintour They were killed with one shot!

The action continues normally. Catherine is visibly upset

Jenny Catherine? Are you all right?
Catherine Wheel Oh I'm just being silly. Robin never would listen to me.
Robert Keyes Well that's about it. The survivors are in the tower now.

As the dialogue continues the main area lights go out and the area is cleared (some soldiers could come on and hoist the bodies off)

When clear the whole stage lights again to represent the rest of the club

Robert Keyes I can't believe the quiet guy talked.
Maggie Oh come on, he spent twelve days in the Tower.
Jenny Most people wouldn't last twelve minutes.
Robert Keyes But he was always so — quiet.
Catherine Wheel It didn't matter anyway. Someone has known about your plot all the way along.
Robert Keyes Who?
Catherine Wheel Speak of the devil…

Cecil enters and sits down at a far table

Robert Keyes curses and hurriedly tries to sneak away

Stay down.

Maggie and Jenny hurriedly give him items of their costume to wear such as a hat or a boa

Maggie Pretend you're one of us.
Catherine Wheel He's on his own, he isn't looking for you.
Robert Keyes There's no way he knew about the plot.
Catherine Wheel When were your servants first arrested?
Robert Keyes November fifth.
Maggie But Fawkes didn't talk until the ninth.
Catherine Wheel See? Cecil already knew who you were.

The Waitress approaches Cecil

Waitress Good-evening and welcome to Catesby's. My name is Denise and I'll be your waitress for this evening. We hope you enjoy your visit.

Cecil quietly orders off the cocktail list as Robert Keyes hisses at Catherine Wheel

Robert Keyes How did he know?
Catherine Wheel I guess it started with a silly mistake.
Robert Keyes Impossible.
Catherine Wheel When Tom Wintour and the other fools were digging that tunnel, they heard a cellar being cleared through the wall.
Robert Keyes So?
Jenny If the diggers heard people in the cellar ——
Maggie — the people in the cellar must have heard the diggers!
Robert Keyes So why weren't they arrested then and there?
Jenny Yes, why not?
Catherine Wheel That's been Cecil's big joke, he's helped you all the way along!
Robert Keyes He helped us?

The Waitress brings Cecil two drinks

Maggie (*noticing the drinks*) Ooh look, he's expecting company.
Robert Keyes What do you mean he was helping us?
Catherine Wheel That house you rented from John Whynniard, convenient wasn't it?

Robert Keyes Yes, that was a real bit of luck.
Catherine Wheel Not for John. He died rather suddenly on the fifth.
Robert Keyes So?
Catherine Wheel So I think John had been ordered to let you have his house.
Maggie And then they topped him to keep his mouth shut.
Robert Keyes Chorus girl gossip. Cecil couldn't have risked it.
Maggie That's nothing.
Jenny Cecil let you have thirty-six barrels of gunpowder!
Robert Keyes He *let* us have it?
Catherine Wheel Well you couldn't just buy it in a shop, could you?
Robert Keyes We bribed some guards in the Tower armoury.
Maggie You're kidding, aren't you?
Jenny You can bribe them if you want to sneak in and see someone ——
Maggie —and for a really big bribe they might leave you alone together—
Jenny — just for a couple of minutes.
Maggie Mind, that's usually long enough.
Catherine Wheel But they'd never give you gunpowder.
Maggie A pocketful maybe ——
Jenny — but thirty-six barrels? Get real!
Catherine Wheel They were told to let you have it.
Jenny Otherwise how could they explain half a store room going empty?
Robert Keyes Nobody realized it had gone.
Catherine Wheel No, not officially, but there's another funny thing. Did you know the records for that month have disappeared and yet nobody seems bothered? Can you imagine Cecil just sitting there saying "forget it, it doesn't matter"?

They watch as The Waitress goes over to Cecil's table

Waitress Sorry, sir, I didn't ask if you wanted ice.
Cecil Forget it. It doesn't matter.
Maggie Doesn't come natural to him, does it?
Jenny You know what? I think he's been stood up.
Robert Keyes Tell me this then. Why would Sir Robert Cecil, the biggest anti-Catholic in the land help us?
Catherine Wheel Because when he first heard about the plot, there were only a few of you involved. He wanted to let it grow and then take out as many Catholics as possible. And he's done it.
Robert Keyes But suppose he hadn't stopped us in time?
Catherine Wheel He knew every move you made.
Robert Keyes How?
Catherine Wheel Francis Tresham's my guess.
Robert Keyes But Francis gave us two thousand pounds, and besides he was arrested.

Catherine Wheel Yes, but he never stood trial, and they never released a statement from him.
Maggie And then he got a fever and died in the Tower.
Catherine Wheel Did he? That was very convenient.
Maggie They quietly chopped him up and chucked him down a hole.
Robert Keyes How do you know?
Maggie I'm friendly with one of the keepers.
Jenny Very friendly, every Thursday afternoon.
Maggie He said the corpse stank something rotten.
Catherine Wheel Which usually means poison.
Robert Keyes No, if he was on their side, why kill him?
Catherine Wheel Good question. Why don't you ask the man over there?
Robert Keyes Not funny.
Jenny Come on, Catherine, you know.
Maggie You always know.
Catherine Wheel Well, it's only a guess, but I think Tresham was a double agent.
Robert Keyes A what?
Catherine Wheel He started on your side, but Cecil found out and blackmailed him. Then in the end Cecil got rid of him because he knew too much.
Jenny But Catherine, how did Cecil find out Tresham was in the plot in the first place?
Catherine Wheel Maybe we'll never know that much.
Maggie Shhh! look at this.

A hooded woman (Lily Gage) comes on to join Cecil

Cecil leaps up to pull a chair out for her, she sits primly. He slides one of the drinks towards her and tries to take her hand in his. She slaps his offered hand and holds out her own hand for payment. Cecil sighs and gives her a little bag which she opens. She tips some gold coins on to her hand and seems satisfied. Cecil tries to take her hand again but she snatches it away

Cecil gives up, wearily rises to his feet and goes

Jenny What was all that about?
Robert Keyes I wonder…

Robert Keyes rises to his feet and crosses to the woman. He pulls back her hood

Lily Gage!

Lily rises and dashes off

Robert Keyes is about to chase her

Oliver and the Puritans dash on

Oliver Robert Keyes?
Robert Keyes Who?
Jenny What do you want?
Oliver We're just mopping up the strays. We got Digby, we got Bates, we're gonna get Wintour, but today we got Keyes.
Jenny Tell them to bog off.
Maggie Except the tall one. Come here, dear, I've been saving myself for you.

Robert Keyes leaps up with his sword. The Puritans leap back, but then Keyes chucks it away. He ponders

Robert Keyes Francis Tresham, the thirteenth man. Funny old world, isn't it?

They go off

The Lights fade to Black-out

Music 24. An instrumental chorus from "The Quiet Guy" is played to cover the scene change

Scene 6

The Tower Cells

The scene could be set by some chains and a barred window and murky lighting

As the Lights come up we see Thomas Wintour, Robert Wintour, Digby, Fawkes, Grant, Rookwood, Keyes, and Bates all sitting mournfully

Robert Wintour Well brother, I told you I'd see you again.
Thomas Wintour You did, Robert. You did.
Digby Look chaps, I don't want to go on about this.
John Grant So don't.
Digby But I still don't quite follow, why did Sir Robin tell me that the King was dead?

John Grant Not again.
Digby The King was right there in the courtroom. He looked pretty alive to me.
Thomas Wintour He should have been dead, and Sir Robin didn't want to disappoint you.
Digby Oh I see. He thought I'd be upset, so he told a lie.
Thomas Wintour Yes.
Digby That was jolly thoughtful of him.
Bates A very gentlemenny man is that gentleman what he was.
John Grant Shouldn't you be in the servants' jail?

Walter Raleigh comes by

Raleigh I say, hallo you chaps!
All Sir Walter!
Digby You're looking well.
Robert Keyes Very well — for a man who was supposed to be executed two years ago.
Raleigh Yes, well King Jimmy decided to let me keep my head as long as I stay here and behave myself.
Robert Wintour But you cruise round like you own the place.
Raleigh They've been pretty decent really. I'm writing poetry and a history of the world. The only thing I miss is a bit of sailing, but there you are.
Digby Do you think King James might let us off too?
John Grant Fat chance. We were plotting to kill him remember?
Digby But he's still alive.
John Grant Yes.
Digby So why did Sir Robin tell me the King was dead?
John Grant Oh not again.

There is a commotion outside. We hear Mrs Fawkes shouting

Mrs Fawkes (*off*) Get out of the way, we're coming in.

Mrs Fawkes, Mrs Wright and Mrs Percy enter with Matthew and Eunice who are looking very harassed

Matthew Please! Our orders are no friends or relatives.
Eunice Not even priests.
Mrs Fawkes Well we're in.
Mrs Percy What you going to do about it?

Raleigh goes to chat to Matthew and Eunice

Raleigh Oh dear, you're in trouble now, chaps.
Matthew But what can we do?
Eunice We'll take 'em round the office.
Matthew We can't go beating up old ladies.
Mrs Fawkes Old? Did he call me old?
Mrs Wright I'm saying nothing.
Raleigh Look chaps, maybe we should just quietly toddle along.
Matthew But …
Raleigh Don't worry. I won't say anything if you don't.
Matthew Thanks, Sir Walter.
Eunice You're a real gent.

Raleigh ushers Matthew and Eunice off

Mrs Fawkes Where's Guy? Hallo, son. So these are all your friends then, these are the great conspirators.

Mrs Fawkes goes to cradle Guy

Mrs Percy Look at them all moping around.
Mrs Fawkes They always mope. I hate it when they mope.
John Grant You'd be moping too if you'd had the trial we had.
Thomas Wintour Sir Edward Coke went into every tiny detail of execution.
John Grant He was loving it. We're to be hung by the neck, then cut down alive.
Thomas Wintour And then they cut us open and pull out all our innards and burn them.
Rookwood While we're still alive.
Mrs Fawkes And you call that punishment?
Mrs Percy You were quite happy to go blowing other people apart, weren't you?
Mrs Fawkes But now we're feeling a bit sorry for ourselves, are we?
Mrs Percy You didn't feel very sorry for all the innocent people you might have killed, did you?
Digby That's not fair! I had some friends that were in danger which I prevented.
John Grant *What*?
Digby My chums Montague, Mordaunt and Stourton, they're frightfully decent coves. I had to let them know.
John Grant You gave us away ——
Rookwood A chap has to do the right thing. Which of us didn't try to save a friend or two?
Robert Keyes Not me.

Bates That's because you haven't got any friends, you miserable git. Sorry your gentlemensies, but it had to be said.
Thomas Wintour Let's face it, the plan should have had a way of saving the Catholic Lords.
Mrs Percy So now it comes out. Anyone of you might have given it away.
Mrs Fawkes Except one. The one who isn't whinging. The one who stood up to the rack for a week. It's no good, Guy, what you tried to do makes me sick to me gizzard. But I'm proud of the way you did it.
Mrs Percy Look at his mates all wetting themselves.
Rookwood But they're going to cut off our privy parts and burn them in front of our faces.
Mrs Wright Won't make much of a barbecue, will it?

They all stare at her

I'm saying nothing.
Mrs Fawkes Did you know people have been writing in with suggestions?
Mrs Percy That Thomas Elliot won it for me ——
Mrs Fawkes Yeah, he'd have you dipped in molten lead ——
Mrs Percy — then stuck on a church roof so the crows can peck you to bits.
Mrs Fawkes Love it.
Thomas Wintour Exactly why did you come visiting?
Mrs Fawkes To offer our sympathies of course.
Mrs Percy No gratitude, have they?
Mrs Fawkes Miserable lot. Listen:

25: Smile As You Go

(*Singing*) Everything that's coming, you deserve it
Mrs Percy I wouldn't spit to save you if I could
Mrs Fawkes What is gonna happen's gonna happen
Mrs Percy So being gutless won't do any good
Both But there's a chance for fame and glory
'Cos how you are remembered will depend
Mrs Fawkes On the valiant glow
Mrs Percy And the pride that you show
Mrs Wright As you're dragged off to your agonizing end.

As the song continues, the Chorus come on in the background

Women You've got to
Smile as you go and step in
Style as you go and
Show the world you just don't care.

With a swing of your hip
And keeping a stiff upper lip
You know it, you owe it
To everyone there.

Chorus So call their bluff as you go and
Strut your stuff as you go
To look your maker in the eye
Women You know bloody well you've
Picked up a ticket to hell
Chorus So bye goodbye goodbye.

But if your a—ta—ta-titude is zero
You'll be going out on your own
But if you act—act—act it like a hero
Then you'll never have to go it alone.

So wave as you go and be
Brave as you go
You might even want to misbehave as you go.

There's no time for crying when you're going to die
So wipe that final tear from your eye
Blow them a kiss 'cos this is for ever
Bye bye.

Robert Wintour They're right.
Conspirators (*speaking*) Eh?
Robert Wintour (*singing*) They've got a point
Thomas Wintour (*speaking*) Robert?
Robert Wintour (*singing*) Don't let your faces, get out of joint.
Mrs Fawkes (*speaking*) Listen to him.
Robert Wintour (*singing*) It has to be the worst day that we'll ever face
But after that we'll end up in a far better place.

Robert Keyes Think it out.
John Grant (*speaking*) Misery?
Robert Keyes What's the cost?
We're born with nothing so what have we lost?
Digby They might cut me up and stick my head on a pole
Conspirators But I'll be damned if I let them interfere with my soul
Chorus Stick out your chin, give 'em a grin
Conspirators The harder that they hit us, the more we can win.

All So smile as you go and step in
Style as you go and
Show the world you just don't care
With a swing of your hip and
Keeping a stiff upper lip
You know it, you owe it
To everyone there.

So call their bluff as you go and
Strut your stuff as you go
To look your maker in the eye
You know bloody well you've
Picked up a ticket to hell
So bye goodbye goodbye.

And if you cry cry cry like a sinner
You've got a judgement day to come
But if you ride ride ride it like a winner
Then you'll always be a star to your mum.

So dare as you go with a
Flare as you go
To stick two fingers in the air as you go
There's no time for crying when you're going to die
Just raise your knee and slap that thigh
Blow them a kiss 'cos this is for ever
Bye bye — bye —bye.

Conspirators So though they send us to meet the great creator
We know they'll have to join us sooner or later
That's the joke
And that's all folks

So bye bye.

SCENE 7

Club Finale

The sign is on. (**For full fireworks option see "staging suggestions" p.80*)

King James, his Groom, Cecil and others come on to inspect the powder barrels

King James So Sir Robert, it's all over.
Cecil Indeed, sire. We're just rounding up and executing some of the priests involved as we speak.
King James And this is the powder that would have finished us all! Doesn't it scare you, Sir Robert?
Cecil Hah! This stuff's so mouldy, you couldn't blow your nose with it.
King James You know, Salisbury, if I was to die, there are worse places than the House of Lords.
Cecil Really?

King James comes to the front and does a posh speech

King James "It should never be spoken or written in ages succeeding that I had died ingloriously in an Ale-house, a Stews, or such vile place, but that mine end should have been with the most honourable and best company."
Groom What are you spouting on like that for?
King James Posterity. Right, I think this calls for a celebration.
Groom Oooh yes, anything for posterity! You, bring that wine in.

On comes Bagwich with some wine in glasses

Bagwich Here. (*To the audience*) Turns out the wine was wanted after all. Well I wasn't to know I'm only the servant.

Bagwich exits

The Groom hands wine out

King James Shame we haven't something nice to go with it.
Cecil How about some of Raleigh's tobacco, sire?
Groom Oh go on, it's all the rage.

The Groom hands James a cigar

King James I'm not hungry.
Groom No, sire! Look, you put it in your mouth and I set fire to the end.
King James Like this?

The Groom lights it up for him (*using a lantern or something*)

Groom There, sire. Now give it a good suck.

James drags then coughs, accidentally bites the end off the cigar then spits

King James This custom is loathsome to ye eye, hateful to ye nose, harmful to ye braine, dangerous to ye lungs and in the black stinking fume thereof, nearest resembling ye horrible Stigian smoke of ye pit that is bottomless.
Groom There's his posterior talking again.
King James One day I really will execute that Walter Raleigh. This smoking could kill a chap.

He tosses the cigar away. It lands by the gunpowder

Absolutely massive bang. Black-out, and the whole place collapses. Everybody exits

26: Cabaret Finale

The Lights gradually come up as the intro starts slowly and quietly

Catherine Wheel comes through the debris. She picks up the odd item and discards it wistfully. As she sings members of the chorus make their way on stage to join her

Catherine W So that was cabaret time down at Catesby's
The bell for last orders just rang.
We've rattled along, we couldn't go wrong
We came in with a song, we went out with a bang.

Chorus We've had a fabaret time down at Catesby's
But the grand finale's in sight

There is a sudden upbeat

You know what they say
Be happy today
The sorrows of tomorrow are a lifetime away
It's fun fun fun fun fun all the way
At Catesby's cabaret.
Catesby's cabaret
Catesby's cabaret
Catesby's cabaret.

Instrumental for walkdown, during which whole cast come on

All So that was cabaret time down at Catesby's
We hope you had a laugh and a thrill

It's one of those shows
Where anything goes
And before we close it probably will.

We had a fabaret time down at Catesby's
Your presence was a total delight
If it wasn't for you, sitting it through
We couldn't do the favourite things we just got to do
So thank you, *danke*, *merci beaucoup*
From Catesby's cabaret ——

There is a long low chord as the Waitress speaks

Waitress Thank you for visiting Catesby's. We hope you found it an enjoyable experience and we look forward to seeing you again soon. Service is not included.

There is a final musical flourish

All Tonight!

STAGING SUGGESTIONS

The Cupboard!

There's all sorts of ways of making the cupboard rock, then the guy appear. Probably the simplest is to have the cupboard to the side of the stage so that it can be rocked by somebody standing off. The cupboard should also have a false back so that the Fawkes dummy (or a replica) can be inserted at the right time. The dummy should be hung from a hook at the front so that when James opens the doors the dummy is right in front of him.

If you can manage it, a more effective way is to have the cupboard on stage away from the wings, but turned slightly to one side. The cupboard will need to be large enough for an operator to stand in the corner. The inside of the cupboard should be painted matt black (or better still draped in black velvet), and the operator should be in black clothes. One or two very brightly coloured items should hang down from a rail. It would also help the operator if the feet of the cupboard were not quite even so he can rock the cupboard from inside. (Be careful that the whole thing doesn't go over!) The Fawkes dummy or a replica should be hidden in a black bag.

When James first opens the cupboard, the operator should stand in the back downstage corner behind one of the coloured items. James flicks through the items rapidly establishing that they are all hanging loose and empty. Of course, when James finally opens the cupboard doors, the operator has got the Guy from the bag, and lunges it out at James.

If you only have a small cupboard and no suitable wings, then the cupboard could be rocked by discreet ropes and poles, or even the chorus could do it. A piece of black velvet should be fixed under the roof of the cupboard to act as a secret "shelf" to hold a dummy replica; this replica does not need any stuffing so that it can fold flat. The head of the replica should be attached to the top of the cupboard. One end of the velvet shelf should be held in place by a peg or other simple device that can be removed from outside the cupboard.

Initially when James looks inside the cupboard, the dummy should remain hidden above the velvet "shelf". Just before the last few lines of the song, one of the chorus removes the peg holding the shelf up — so the dummy will flop down and hang behind the door waiting for James to discover it.

Remember — whatever you do the audience should not be expecting it so hopefully you'll give them all a good jump!

The Rack Illusion

One way to do this is to have a replica Fawkes dummy lying on a table. The sleeves and trouser legs are much longer than the original, but tucked up so that initially the dummy looks in the same proportions as usual.

Ropes are tied to the feet and arms. You could have the free ends of the ropes attached to capstans similar to a traditional rack, but it's up to you how gruesome you want the whole thing to look. When the ropes are first pulled, they should hardly move, and the pullers should look like they are putting a huge effort in. Very slowly though, let the dummy get longer and longer!

A completely unmacabre version, and one which might help your audience see better, involves the dummy having telescopic legs. The trouser legs of the dummy should each have a cardboard roll down them, then inside each roll you put a pole with a foot on the end. The poles could have some sort of long socks on. This way the feet and legs can be slid in and out of the trousers. You could even have the poles initially going right up inside the body, so that when the legs are be extended they can come out to over an extra metre in length. The dummy should then be mounted vertically, hanging by his arms from two ropes over high pulleys. Initially the dummy is at normal height to the floor so that the legs are the expected length. However, when the ropes are pulled, the dummy will rise into the air, but his legs will seem to extend! Of course this gives some extra comic value if William Waad needs to climb a ladder to hear the dummy "speak".

A Thousand Angry Men

Obviously in this scene the people in the club are hearing about what happened to the conspirators — but it might need to be made clear on stage that the enactment takes place in a different location. A simple suggestion is that rather than having the full stage lights up representing the club, during the enactment there is a small pool of light on Catherine and co., then the rest of the stage is lit up very differently — either in a single deep colour such as red, or from beneath by footlights which would give a suitably eerie effect, especially with big shadows going up and down as they mime riding their horses. The lighting of course should return to normal when the enactment finishes as detailed in the script.

Fireworks Option!

It may be desirable to tie the production in with an outdoor fireworks display to round the show off. All you need to do is after the "Smile As You Go" song finishes, you bring on King James, Cecil and the Groom.

King James So, Sir Robert, it's all over?
Cecil Indeed, sire. We're just rounding up and executing some of the priests involved as we speak.
King James You know, after everything, I have a fascination to see this powder that could have destroyed us. Where is it now?
Cecil Outside, sire.
King James Come on then. Let's have a look.

King James and everybody go outside, followed by the audience! The thirty-six barrels are assembled by the fireworks area

Once outside and everybody is assembled safely ——

So this is the powder that would have finished us all! Doesn't it scare you, Sir Robert?
Cecil Hah! This stuffs so mouldy, you couldn't blow your nose with it.

Continue scene as written in the text, but when James chucks his cigar, your fireworks start, then the cast come on for an outdoor Finale at the end

There are just two points if you do the fireworks option — first *please* make absolutely sure it is properly organized and safe, and second, please contact the author (in other words me) because I'd love to see it!

Kjartan Poskitt

FURNITURE AND PROPERTY LIST

Further dressing may be added at the director's discretion

ACT I

CATESBY'S CABARET CLUB

On stage: Trick table. *On it*: long cloth
Tables with chairs
Broken chairs
Pieces of abandoned clothing
Sword embedded in back wall (optional)
Lanterns
Piece of pie

Off stage: Chair with full size, fully clothed traditional Guy Fawkes dummy (**Mrs Fawkes**)
King James's glass (**Waitress**)
Bag covered in travel labels (**Garnet**)
Papers (**Robert Cecil**)
Plan of the gunpowder plot (**Stage Management**)
Gunpowder barrels (**Conspirators**)
Sacks with sticks attached (**Conspirators**)
Fuses (**Conspirators**)

Personal: **Baby**: crown, rattle
Raleigh: chip
Garnet: dark glasses
Thomas Percy: piece of paper
Mounteagle: napkin
Bagwich: piece of paper

KING JAMES'S BOUDOIR

On stage: Cupboard
Bed. *On it*: sheets, pillows, blankets

Off stage: Curtains (**Chorus**)
Chair (**Chorus**)
Teddy (**Chorus**)
Fawkes dummy or replica (**Stage Management**)

ACT II

On stage: Chair. *On it*: Fawkes dummy tied up
Large cloth over plot equipment

Off stage: Frying pan (**Garnet**)
Apron (**Garnet**)
Wrist binding (**Dorothy**)
Cupboard (**Stage Management**)
Bricks (**Stage Management**)
Buckets of cement/building stuff (**Mary** and **Jack**)
King James's writing equipment (**Stage Management**)
Nasty looking implement (**Waad**)
Spread-eagled dummy tied with ropes (**Stage Management**)
Robert Keyes's drink (**Waitress**)
"To Let" sign (**Garnet**)
Cocktail list (**Waitress**)
Two drinks for **Cecil** (**Waitress**)
Chains (optional)
Tray containing wine in glasses (**Bagwich**)

Personal: **Groom**: **King James**'s comb
Waad: letter
Catesby: note
John Wright: sword
Chris Wright: sword
Cecil: small money bag containing gold coins
Robert Keyes: sword
Groom: cigar

LIGHTING PLOT

Practical fittings required: "Catesby's" sign, lanterns.
Various interior and exterior settings.

ACT I, Scene 1. Night

To open: Overall general lighting on Club. "Catesby's" sign is lit. House lights go off as **Eunice** and **Matthew** enter

Cue 1 **Garnet**: "Got it in one my son." (Page 7)
Fade to black-out

ACT I, Scene 2

To open: Bring up lights on **Mrs Fawkes**'s living-room

Cue 2 **Mrs Wright**: "I'm saying nothing." (Page 9)
Cross-fade to Club lighting. "Catesby's" sign on

ACT I, Scene 3

Cue 3 **Catherine Wheel**: "… late for the dream sequence." (Page 20)
Fade to black-out

ACT I, Scene 4. Late night

To open: Bring up lights on **King James**'s bedroom

Cue 4 Big chord (Page 25)
Black-out

ACT I, Scene 5

To open: Bring up Club lighting. Snap on "Catesby's" sign

Cue 5 They look at **Catesby** aghast (Page 27)
Fade to black-out

Cue 6 When ready (Page 27)
Lights fade up as before on Club

Cue 7 **Catesby** exits (Page 30)
Fade to black-out

ACT I, SCENE 6

To open: Bring up general lighting on Parlour

Cue 8 **Cecil**: "… might self-destruct." (Page 31)
Fade to black-out

ACT I, SCENE 7

To open: Bring up Club lighting. Snap on "Catesby's" sign

Cue 9 **Dorothy** runs off (Page 39)
Black-out

ACT I, SCENE 8

To open: Bring up general lighting on Mounteagle's House

Cue 10 **Mounteagle**: "… of your friends ——" (Page 40)
Fade to black-out

ACT I, SCENE 9

To open: Lights up on **Mounteagle**

Cue 11 The **Groom** exits (Page 42)
Fade to black-out

ACT I, SCENE 10

To open: When ready bring up Cellar lighting

Cue 12 **Cecil**: "… where the party really starts." (Page 45)
Fade to black-out

ACT II, SCENE 1

To open: Dim lighting on Fawkes in the Tower

Cue 13 The **Chorus** enter (Page 46)
Lighting brightens

Cue 14 **Chorus**: "'Cos he's just one hell of a guy." (Page 48)
Black-out

ACT II, SCENE 2

To open: Bring up Club lighting. Snap on "Catesby's" sign

Cue 15 **Jenny**: "… believed me do you?" (Page 50)
Black-out

ACT II, SCENE 3

To open: Bring up shadowy lighting

Cue 16 The last brick goes in (Page 53)
Fade to black-out

ACT II, SCENE 4

To open: Bring up lighting on the King's Boudoir

Cue 17 **King James**: "… to Sir William Waad." (Page 56)
Fade to black-out

ACT II, SCENE 5

To open: Snap on "Catesby's" sign. Bring up dim lighting on **Matthew** and **Eunice**

Cue 18 **Catherine Wheel** enters (Page 56)
Bring up spot on **Catherine Wheel**

Cue 19 When ready
Cut spot on **Catherine Wheel.** *Bring up general lighting* (Page 56)

Cue 20 The song ends (Page 58)
Reduce lighting to a small pool on **Catherine Wheel**, **Jenny** *and* **Maggie**

Cue 21 **Robert Keyes**: "… quite a force organized." (Page 59)
Bring up main area lighting on **Conspirators**

Cue 22 **Catesby**: "We'll stop at Holbeach and rest up." (Page 62)
Lights alter to indoor night-time effect

Cue 23 The **Conspirators** scream (Page 62)
Bring up outdoor daylight effect on main area

Cue 24 **Catherine Wheel**: "Wind it back." (Page 64)
Lights flicker on main area

Cue 23 **Robert Keyes**: "The survivors are in the Tower now." (Page 65)
Fade main area lighting. When ready bring up Club lighting overall. Snap on "Catesby's" sign

Cue 24 They exit with **Robert Keyes** (Page 69)
Fade to black-out

ACT II, SCENE 6

To open: Murky lighting on Tower cells

No cues

ACT II, SCENE 7

To open: Bring up Club lighting. Snap on "Catesby's" sign

Cue 25 Absolutely massive bang (Page 76)
Black-out

Cue 26 Intro to "Cabaret Finale" (Page 76)
Gradually bring up Club lighting

EFFECTS PLOT

ACT I

No cues

ACT II

Cue 1	**Catherine Wheel**: "Well?" *Flash or small bang* (optional)	(Page 62)
Cue 2	**Chris Wright**: "… so let's si' thee." *Two shots*	(Page 64)
Cue 3	**Rookwood**: "… a chap simply does not do …" *Shot*	(Page 64)
Cue 4	**Catesby**: "Sing up, you men!" *Shot*	(Page 64)
Cue 5	**Catesby**: "Sing up, you men!" *Shot*	(Page 65)
Cue 6	**King James** tosses the cigar away *Absolutely massive bang*	(Page 76)